C000157012

MASTERING
HOMEBREW
THE BEER MAKER'S BIBLE

MASTERING
HOMEBREW
THE BEER MAKER'S BIBLE

Brian Kunath

APPLE

A QUINTET BOOK

Published by The Apple Press
6 Blundell Street
London N7 9BH

Copyright © 1998 Quintet Publishing Limited.
All rights reserved. No part of this publication may be
reproduced, stored in a retrieval system or transmitted
in any form or by any means, electronic, mechanical,
photocopying, recording, or otherwise, without the
permission of the copyright holder.

ISBN 1-85076-991-5

This book was designed and produced by
Quintet Publishing Limited
6 Blundell Street
London N7 9BH

Creative Director: Richard Dewing
Project Editor: Clare Hubbard
Editor: Andrew Armitage
Designer: Peter Laws
Photographer: Keith Waterton/Jeremy Thomas

Typeset in Great Britain by
Central Southern Typesetters, Eastbourne
Manufactured in Singapore by Bright Arts Pte Ltd.
Printed in China by Leefung-Asco Printers Ltd.

Picture Credits
Pgs 10, 11, E. T. Archive; pg 40 Life File; pg 45 Heather Angel.

Conversion
The imperial liquid quantities (gallons, quarts, pints) in this book are US measures
which differ from UK measures;

i.e. 1 US gallon = 3.8 litres while 1 UK gallon = 4.5 litres

If you prefer to brew using UK gallons/quarts/pints, multiply the metric litre
quantities by 0.22.

e.g 2.5 litres x 0.22 = 0.55 gallons (4 pints)
or 800 ml = convert to 0.8 litres then multiply by 0.22 = 0.176 gallons
When converting measures be sure to convert all measures and follow
throughout the whole recipe otherwise the proportions of the ingredients could be
critically imbalanced.

Publisher's Note
All statements, information, and advice given in this book regarding methods and
techniques are believed to be true and accurate. The author, copyright holders, and
the publisher cannot accept any legal liability for errors or omissions.

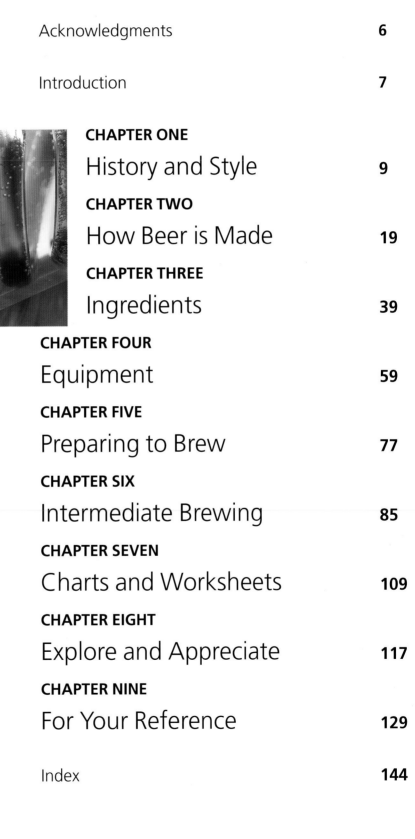

Contents

Acknowledgments   **6**

Introduction   **7**

CHAPTER ONE

History and Style   **9**

CHAPTER TWO

How Beer is Made   **19**

CHAPTER THREE

Ingredients   **39**

CHAPTER FOUR

Equipment   **59**

CHAPTER FIVE

Preparing to Brew   **77**

CHAPTER SIX

Intermediate Brewing   **85**

CHAPTER SEVEN

Charts and Worksheets   **109**

CHAPTER EIGHT

Explore and Appreciate   **117**

CHAPTER NINE

For Your Reference   **129**

Index   **144**

Acknowledgments

I COULDN'T HAVE WRITTEN THIS BOOK without help and so I'd like to express my appreciation to those who gave their time, expertise, and support during the various stages of this book. Without exception, the people I met and sought council from have been enthusiastic and generous.

First, I'd like to thank Scott Youmans and all the guys at Pinehurst Brewery for giving up time and space for countless questions and some fine photographs. Stephen Snyder helped me get this book published and gave me valuable guidance whenever I needed it. I also want to thank all of the folks at American Brewmaster, who let me barge in and borrow equipment, take photographs, and solicit advice.

Glenn Tinseth generously allowed me to use his hops charts and formulas for the book. Chris Russell of New York Homebrew and Lynne O'Conner of St. Patrick's of Texas Brewing Supply, both gave advice and homebrew recipes. Other recipe contributors include Peter A'Hearn from the Homebrew Mart, Marci from Maui Home Brew Supply, Jim McHale and Lisa Budduck from Beer Unlimited, Jim Tesch from Double Springs Homebrew Supply, and the folks at Alfred's Brewing Supply.

Thanks also to Keith Waterton for his patience, perseverance, and good sense of humor. Also, to Clare Hubbard, Diana Steedman, and Richard Dewing. I'd also like to thank my agent, Mark Ryan, for helping to guide me through my first book.

I'd be "Beerlessly Stewing" if it weren't for authors and homebrew kingpins Charlie Papazian, Byron Burch, Dave Miller, Randy Mosher, and Ray Daniels.

In addition, I want to thank those who supported me in this endeavor. This includes my girlfriend, Pamela, my mom and dad, and my sister Kristen. Finally, thanks to David Fifield for helping me get started and my brother, Tom, for introducing me to all this crazy homebrewing stuff in the first place.

This book is dedicated to my grandmother. Nana: here's the one book you've yet to read, about the only craft you've never tried.

Introduction

I BREWED MY FIRST BATCH OF BEER on Christmas day in 1990. My brother, Tom, gave me a basic kit, along with some ingredients and a slim volume written by Byron Burch entitled, Brewing Quality Beers. I stumbled through the first batch, following my brother's instructions yet having no idea what I was doing. I washed and sanitized, mixed, stirred, and boiled, and pitched a packet of dry yeast into the pungent concoction that Tom referred to as "wert." A couple of weeks later I had two cases of weizen.

Intrigued by my homebrew success—though I still had no clue as to what exactly my role had been—I decided to read Burch's book. I made a few more batches, some good, others "drinkable." I kept the better efforts for gatherings and parties. I'd distribute a dozen chilled bottles to friends, give them a brief seminar on homebrew pouring technique, and watch their eyes for feedback. Most of my macrobrew-drinking buddies finished one glass and went back to their beer of choice. However, I did make a few converts to the world of specialty beer. I was satisfied with my technique. Then I brewed a batch so awful that the only thing fit to swallow it was the kitchen sink.

My illusion of being a brewmaster had vanished. The thrill was gone, along with about twenty bucks worth of ingredients, literally down the drain. What had gone wrong? The truth is, I didn't know. In fact, I knew little about how to brew beer except that you put some ingredients in a pot and mixed them together. I re-read Burch's book. I bought more books. I decided to actually learn how malt, hops, water, and yeast conspired to transform "wert" into beer. The more I read, the more I realized that while the science behind brewing is very complex, the craft of making consistently good beer is fairly simple and straightforward.

This is a book that addresses the mistakes I made as a novice homebrewer. All of the things I overlooked are explored here in detail. Each of the suggestions I initially ignored in other texts are stressed in this book. There are four basic concepts that, if understood and followed, will ensure great beer every time. These are:

1. Maintaining sanitary conditions
2. Following proper procedure
3. Keeping a detailed journal for each batch of homebrew
4. Understanding the art and science of brewing

This book explores each of these ideas and offers a bit more. There is a chapter that details cleaning and sanitation of your equipment and work area. I have included Homebrew Charts to organize each batch of beer you brew, and to help you predict how your homebrew will turn out. These charts serve as a map and a journal. I recommend the use of a notebook and a calculator to be used in conjunction with the charts. There are also sections that delve lightly into the science behind brewing to help you understand what is going on in the brewpot.

I have tried to write a book that will lure the curious, calm the clueless, and quickly guide the novice toward intermediate procedures and, more importantly, great homebrew. So whether you like porter or pilsner, weizen or witbier, or bock or barley wine, fear not. Successful brewing is right around the corner.

CHAPTER ONE

History and Style

A stylish history

GEOGRAPHY, TRADE, ECONOMICS, and social climate have all influenced the emergence of major beer styles. Beer, in one form or another, has been with humanity for over 8,000 years. Like the adaptive nature of human beings, beer has changed with climate. And as people have forged civilization, trade routes, and technological advancement, beer has always been close at hand, mirroring the evolution of societies around the world.

Beer has been both scion of scientific discovery and patron to its progress. For example, Louis Pasteur was studying the causes of beer spoilage in the mid-nineteenth century. He found that if during the brewing process wort (unfermented beer) was raised to a high temperature and then cooled quickly, a great number of microorganisms would be eliminated. Thus, he increased the shelf life of beer. This process was tested in the dairy industry with great success. Where untreated milk soured, harboring bacteria that caused typhoid and tuberculosis, pasteurized milk was stripped of such pathogens. To this day, most prepackaged food goes through the same process. Historically, new medicines and inventions have often crept from the work of men and women striving toward unrelated goals. If serendipity has played a part in the progressive application of scientific inquiry, then it is fitting that the "invention" of beer probably came as a desperate experiment to remedy an accident.

▲ *Louis Pasteur, whose research into yeast activity was vital to increasing the shelf life of beer.*

Origins

Most likely, an ancient Sumerian farmer left a crop of cut barley out in a rainstorm. In an effort to save his resource from rot, he may have laid the grain out in the sun to dry. Barley was an important food source in early civilization, so any substantial loss could prove disastrous for a family or community. By exposing the barley to water and then allowing it to dry under a hot Mesopotamian sun, this farmer would have produced "malt." Upon tasting the barley, he would have found it sweeter and easier to chew. A gruel or bread made with malt would taste better than that made with raw barley, as hard starches within the grain are converted into sugars as malt is produced. Soon, or perhaps much later, a bread or cake made of malted barley may have been exposed to further rainwater. This wet mixture may then have been host to airborne wild yeast. Fermentation would result, and any liquid squeezed from the bread would be beer. One can imagine the unprecedented sense of euphoria the Sumerians must have felt upon sampling this elixir. How could they account for the inexplicable? Beer is a natural product composed of elements from both sky and earth. Indeed, early civilizations surmised as much, but credited spiritual, not scientific, sources for the creation of beer.

The ancients regarded beer as a gift from the gods. The Sumerian goddess of beer was called Ninkasi: "The lady who fills the mouth." Egyptian hieroglyphics depict the process of brewing as early as the Fifth Dynasty. Their gods of brewing and beer were Hathor and Seth. The Romans, who regarded beer as an inferior beverage, still bestowed respect for the "grain wine." While Bacchus was praised as the god of wine, Ceres, the goddess of agriculture, was said to impart her strength (in Latin, "*vis*") upon those who drank beer. *Cervesa*, the Spanish word for beer, has its roots in this Latin designation.

Just when mankind stumbled upon the fermented barley beverage remains a mystery. Shards of pottery dating c. 3500–3100 BC have been excavated from sites in the mountains of western Iraq. Grooves within some of these remnants have been found to contain the hardened residue of beer. The use of such jugs, along with other empirical data, suggests that beer was already a dietary staple among the people of Mesopotamia. Clay tablets found in the same region depict groups of people drinking beer from a jug through long straws forged from gold. These tablets have been carbon-dated as far back as 4000 BC.

Most historians believe that beer has a much longer history with mankind, perhaps even prompting the shift from nomadic hunting and gathering to agricultural civilization. However, theories that attempt to pinpoint the birth of beer abound, and rebound off divergent beliefs. Archaeologists have traced the study of various types of barley as far back as 6000 BC. This would indicate a fairly sophisticated understanding of the grain. In fact most historians believe that barley was being used for the production of bread and/or beer two to three thousand years prior to this.

▲ *A painted limestone figure of a female brewer kneading dough for beer; Giza, end of the Fifth Dynasty.*

Early brewers

In most ancient societies, the lofty task of brewing beer was bestowed upon women. Sumerian and Babylonian priestesses were the only people allowed to brew. In Egypt the woman of the house directed the brewing process. Egyptian women created many styles of beer that were rationed to workers, and even exported. The Vikings also gave the task of brewing to women. Both men and women drank heavily in this society. The nomadic Norsemen brought beer to each land they terrorized and plundered. The Vikings believed that after death, they would enter Valhalla, where Odin (or Woden) would entertain them with tales of battles during long drinking sessions.

European brewing

The influence of earlier societies seeped into Europe. The Anglo-Saxons settled into northern Europe after the Romans receded. A large variety of fermented beverages sated the appetites of the nomadic Anglo-Saxons. They used whatever was available–grains, honey, bog myrtle, and a host of other herbs and spices. One popular drink was mead, a honey-fermented, spiced beverage.

Malted barley was used as the chief ingredient of beer in many parts of Europe. Records show that hops, previously a flavoring additive among many other herbs and spices, were used with some consistency in Bavarian beer after the eighth century AD. After the Norman Conquest, Europe became united under the Roman Catholic Church. The Church quickly regulated the production of beer. Monks were allowed to brew, first for personal consumption, and later to support the abbeys. The erudite monks refined brewing practices. In fact, it may have been the monks who first started using hops regularly as a preservative in ale. While the monks praised God for the magic transference of wort to beer, they understood that the hop plant helped to stabilize beer, and thus applied early science to brewing.

Early lagers

Up until the fifteenth century, all beers produced were ales. Since ales are fermented at relatively warm temperatures, they are susceptible to bacterial contaminants, which also favor warm temperatures. Since little was known of microbiology, brewers had to learn or experience empirically that brewing in the summer (when airborne wild yeast and bacteria are at high levels) was a dicey prospect. Therefore, most brewing took place during the fall and winter months.

Bavarians in the 1400s began creating lager beer by placing fermentation vessels in the cold caves of the Alps in early March. They soon realized that the beer could be stored safely throughout the summer, and into the fall when the last reserves were drunk during a festival in October. These early lagers may have hosted strains of yeast that could function at very low temperatures. Since these yeast strains could thrive at temperatures as low as 1°C (34°F) the beer would ferment. Lees (yeast sediment) taken from these batches may have been the first "cultivated" lager yeast.

Quality control

The next milestone in European brewing came in 1516, when Bavaria enacted the *Reinheitsgebot*–a purity law designed to protect the consumer from overpricing and poorly crafted beer. The law stated that the only ingredients allowed to be used for the brewing of beer were barley, hops, and water. Wheat was also allowed, as was yeast–which had yet to be understood by any society. Most German brewers stick to the archaic code to this day, despite competition from mass-produced, high-adjunct lager imports.

Science soothes the wild yeast

In the 1800s, a German scientist, Theodore Schwann, armed with a microscope, proposed that yeast fermentation was a living process. Pasteur later confirmed this observation. Fermentation was indeed the work of living microorganisms, much like the bacteria that fed off meat and milk. Science uncovered what had been a mystery for millennia. The proof was in the pasteurization. Prometheus had finally stolen the magical fermentation process from divine hands.

In the late 1800s, the Danish scientist Emil Hansen isolated two important strains of yeast. The first was *Saccharomyces cerevesiae*, the ale yeast that had been used for up to ten thousand years. The other was *Saccharomyces carlsbergensis* (now *S. uvarum*), which was named after the Carlsberg brewery in Denmark. This major scientific leap improved methods of brewing enormously.

Assembly-line brewing

The Industrial Revolution brought mass marketing to the brewing world. While prohibition had effectively snuffed out most regional breweries in the United States, Britain was slowly being taken over by large breweries that economically bullied local taverns into using their products. After prohibition ended in America, large breweries produced light lagers almost exclusively. The two countries faced a similar dilemma. Some British citizens formed a consumer organization called CAMRA (CAMpaign for Real Ale), which promoted homebrewing as a reaction against the "Big Six" breweries who had invaded local pubs. Americans began homebrewing in the 1970s, once students returning from European tours realized that there was an enormous variety of quality beer available in other countries. In 1979, Congress legalized

▲ *Improved kilning and refrigeration methods coincided with improvements in the quality of glassware. This combination helped a small Bohemian brewery in Plzen to show off its handsome golden lager. Hence, Pilsner Urquell soon became world famous as the first brewery to produce light, clear beer.*

homebrewing in the US. Around the same time, the homebrew pioneer and guru Charlie Papazian created the American Homebrewer's Association, a nonprofit organization that educated homebrewers on the latest homebrewing techniques.

The rebirth of tradition

During the past decade, beer has enjoyed a renaissance. No longer a homogeneous drink imbibed by the "unsophisticated," beer is rightfully taking its place next to wine as a versatile, complex, and delicious beverage. Microbreweries and brewpubs across America have revived old and forgotten recipes from around the world. Today, there are over a million people homebrewing in the United States alone. In Britain CAMRA has succeeded in bringing real "cask-conditioned" ale back into local pubs. The brewing revolution is stronger than ever. Men and women who began as homebrewers head many small breweries. There is a wonderful synergy between microbrewers and homebrewers. The former offer an array of quality beer for the hobbyist to sample and emulate. To use an appropriate metaphor, these breweries provide grist for the mill. In turn, many homebrewers are inspired to refine their craft, perhaps even aspiring toward professional brewing. All of this activity has ignited the creativity of millions. Who knows where the next style will come from?

▲ *During the past decade beer has enjoyed a renaissance, with homebrewing becoming a popular hobby the world over.*

Beers of the world

THE FOLLOWING IS a listing of many major beer styles. While most countries of the world produce beer in some form, this list concentrates on beer produced in Europe and North America.

Ales

Ales use top-fermenting yeast strains to ferment sugars in the wort. Because ale yeast (*Saccharomyces cerevisiae*) quickly ferments wort at warmer temperatures, certain by-products are produced. Many of these help define certain styles of ale.

BELGIUM

Belgian Strong Ales–There are light and dark varieties of this ale, which runs from a pale amber to burgundy and even a deep brown color. These are potent, heavily malted beers with low hopping rates. Strong ales are colored with candi sugar, which can produce vinous notes, along with a warming sensation on the tongue, associated with the high alcohol content.

Belgian Red–This is a very tart light- to medium-bodied ale, which is often fermented with multiple yeast strains. Vienna malt provides the reddish color. Belgian red is often aged in uncoated oak tuns for up to two years. Hopping rates are low.

Flanders Brown–The color of this ale is copper to brown. There is a slight sourness to this beer, along with a fruity, spicy palate. A low diacetyl (butterscotch) flavor is acceptable. Bitterness is low to medium, though there is no hop aroma or flavor.

Lambic–These famous ales are produced in the Senne Valley, where indigenous wild yeasts are allowed to settle on the wort from open slats in the roof of the brewery. The result is an intense, cleanly sour beer. Lambic is made from malted barley and up to 40 percent unmalted wheat. Stale hops are used to help stabilize flavor without imparting bitterness, flavor, or aroma. Lambics are pale in color with some cloudiness.

Kriek (cherry lambic)

- **Faro**–This lambic is refermented with sugar and/or caramel. Faro retains the trademark sour flavor of a lambic, but a subtle sweetness and a soft, rounded palate subdue this.
- **Gueuze**–This very dry lambic is the product of old and young lambic blends. It is very pale in color with little or no diacetyl.
- **Framboise**–This is a raspberry-flavored lambic, dominated by an intensely tart aroma and flavor.

Belgian Pale–Similar to an English pale ale, but the malt profile is a bit more complex due to the mixing in of candi sugar and other additives. Also, Belgian pales are hopped at a much lower rate, highlighting soft fruit and diacetyl notes.

Trappist Ales–These ales are an "Appellation," in that they can be called a Trappist Ale only in the six monasteries where they are brewed. Five of these breweries–Orval, Chimay, Westmalle, Rochefort and Westvleteren–are located in Belgium. The other, Shaapskooi, is located in the Netherlands. These highly esteemed, bottle-conditioned ales come in three general substyles. The house beer has the lightest body. The Dubbel has a medium to full body, and a color that ranges from copper to brown. The flavor is sweet and may have subtle diacetyl undertones. The malt imparts a nutty aroma, and moderate hopping rates may lend a slight hop aroma. The Trippel is the most potent of the three. However, its pale color may surprise and educate those who associate dark color with alcoholic strength.

Wit or **White**–This ale comprises malted barley and unmalted wheat. Witbier is pale and cloudy, and is often spiced with orange peel and coriander. Some estery and diacetyl flavors are acceptable. Hopping rates are low to medium.

THE BRITISH ISLES

Barley Wine–The name comes from the winelike alcoholic potency, not the flavor. Barley wines have an immense malt

profile. The sweetness is often matched by high hopping rates. The color of this ale ranges from amber to copper. Fruity, estery, and diacetyl notes may be apparent. Unlike most ales, barley wine improves dramatically with age.

Bitter—This self-descriptive beer actually resembles traditional IPAs more closely than IPAs produced in Britain today. The color is golden to copper, with a light to medium body. The low malt flavor is outbalanced by higher hopping rates. Cask-conditioned bitters have the low carbonation that is characteristic of this storage and serving method.

Brown Ale—British brown ale and British mild both fall under this category. Brown ale is sweet and full-bodied, with low hop bitterness and aroma. The mild is a lighter-bodied version of the brown, though it may be darker. Brown ales have higher ester and diacetyl levels, which become more pronounced when the beer is served at cellar temperatures.

IPA—India pale ale was originally produced for English colonists in India. To survive the long trip, brewers concocted a high-gravity ale that was aggressively hopped, to promote stability. Though originally produced in London, the hard waters of Burton upon Trent proved a more favorable match to the heavy hop additions. Current British examples replicate the medium body and copper color of the original, but lack the alcoholic strength, bitterness, and hop aroma of the traditional IPA.

Pale Ale—This classic ale is considered pale only in relation to milds, porters, and stouts. Pale ale is actually reddish to copper in color. Similar to bitter ale, pales are well-hopped, though tend to be maltier and more complex, with estery and diacetyl notes that vary among brands.

Porter—Originally called "entire," porters may have been a blend of three styles. Only recently has this defunct style been resurrected, but the modern porter may not resemble the original. Today porter is characterized by a deep brown color with perhaps a tinge of amber if held against a light source. Generally, porters should be full-bodied with a malty sweetness balanced by a sharp bitterness of black malt. Hopping rates range from

Brown ale

medium to high, but no hop aroma or flavor should be present. Fruity, estery, and diacetyl notes may further characterize the modern porter.

Scottish Ales—These are a loose interpretation of the bitter to be found elsewhere in Britain. However, as the cold climate in Scotland hinders hop cultivation, the emphasis is on malt characteristics. Traditional Scottish ales exhibit a smoky flavor from the process of heating green malt over piles of burning peat. Light Scottish ales are gold to amber in color, medium-bodied, and lightly hopped. Scottish "heavy" ales tend to be darker, richer ales, with emphasis on malt complexity. As low-hopped ales, they exhibit more pronounced notes of fruit and butterscotch. Scottish exports are heavier still, while retaining the characteristics of the Scottish heavy. Scotch ale, also known as "wee heavy," is typically more potent than Scottish ales, and is often served in smaller glassware. The malt profile is very complex, exhibiting distinct notes of fruit and butterscotch on the palate.

Stout—A direct descendant of the porter, stouts retain many of its characteristics but add specialty malts, more hops, and various other ingredients that put this style in a class of its own. As a general rule, stouts tend to be darker in color than porter, and proffer roasted coffee notes due to the addition of high-kilned, unmalted barley. The name stout implies a big hearty beer, but this moniker might better serve to illustrate the wide variance of sub-styles that exist within the general category. Stouts have been toyed and tinkered with for many years. Ingredients ranging from whey and milk sugar to molasses and even oysters have been added to stouts. Boiled to the essence, stouts may be divided into the following three categories:

- **Dry Stout**—This style was perfected in Ireland, and continues to be the country's premier export. Dry stouts tend to be black and opaque. The dry flavor is due to the addition of roasted unmalted barley, which offsets the sweetness of other malt additions. High-bittering hop rates provide further balance; however, there is no hop flavor or aroma. The overall flavor of dry stout starts with a malt sweetness and finishes with dry coffee-like flavors. The body ranges from light to medium, and alcohol content is relatively low.

- **Sweet Stout**–Decreased unmalted grain additions, as well as the introduction of lactose, chocolate malt, and sometimes gelatinized oats, make this style of beer sweeter and fuller-bodied than its dry cousin. The color and hop bitterness are the same as in dry stout. Sweet stouts are generally low in alcohol content.

- **Imperial Stout**–This style came as the result of a trade contract between eighteenth-century England and the Russian court. English breweries made stouts for the Russian court but had to prepare the brew for a long journey. Thus, they crafted a high-gravity, highly hopped brew. The brew would complete fermentation en route, and the hops served to protect the beer from developing contaminants. The result was a huge brew: full-bodied, copper to black, highly alcoholic, and rich with fruity esters and hop flavor and aroma.

Strong Ale/English Old Ale–The name "old ale" originally designated mild ales that had been aged in oak barrels for a year or more, and "strong ale" describes the result. Prolonged maturation boosts alcoholic potency, "strengthening" these dark, rich ales. Fruity, estery notes are evident, and diacetyl is medium to high. While these ales are moderately hopped, it is the complex malt profile and warming potency that lingers on the tongue.

FRANCE

Bière de Garde–These ales are produced in Northern France, along the border of Belgium. Several malts and a long maturation in cellars produce a smooth, rich fruity beer. Bière de garde is typically corked, like wine or champagne, rather than capped. The color ranges from golden to a reddish brown. The flavor and aromatic notes vary among breweries, but the long cellaring that is typical of all examples, provides a noticeable warming on the palate.

Bière de Mars–Traditionally this ale was brewed in late fall using malt from the Champagne region of France, to be ready in

Altbier

March to celebrate the arrival of spring. These blond ales are malty and potent, yet smooth on the palate.

GERMANY

Alt–In German "Altbier" means old beer, a designation for ales that have been fermented at warm temperatures using top-fermenting yeast and then lagered at cold temperatures for extended periods of time. The cold storage minimizes the production of esters and diacetyl. While alt may have some fruitiness, moderate hopping rates impart a good portion of the flavor profile.

Dunkelweizen–The name means literally "dark wheat," and these use dark malt to achieve a deep copper color. Wheat is also used, along with a special yeast strain that produces notes of banana and clove. Low hopping rates make this a smooth, sweet brew with an interesting finish.

Hefe-weizen–As with most German wheat beers, these are produced in southern Germany. The combination of malted barley and wheat results in a light, somewhat cloudy ale, with the predominant clove and banana aromas dominating the nose and palate. These beers are unfiltered, leaving yeast sediment at the bottom of the bottle. Devotees of this style swirl the bottle to rouse the yeast into suspension, bringing added complexity to the flavor and mouth-feel.

Weizen–These beers are similar to Hefe-weizen, but are filtered to remove the yeast. Again, wheat is used to up to 60 percent of the grain. These ales range in color, but all are highly carbonated and crystal clear. Special yeast strains impart notes of fruit and spice.

Weizenbock–Bocks are typically dark, potent lagers, but this variant is fermented with top-fermenting yeast at ale temperatures. Weizenbock is typically darker than other German wheat beers, and has a higher alcohol content.

NORTH AMERICA

While light, relatively indistinguishable lagers continue to dominate the American market, craft breweries are reviving European recipes, while putting a distinctly American stamp on certain styles. Hops from the Pacific Northwest, as well as American-grown grains, are often favored by microbreweries for the unique qualities they lend to traditional styles of beer. The American brewer's love affair with the aromatic Cascade hop, for example, has been proven by its use in a number of American interpretations of European styles.

American Amber–This moniker is rapidly becoming a designation for any medium-bodied beer that encompasses various shades of red. Estery and balanced with bittering and aromatic hops, these ales may well become the most popular specialty beer choice among the general public.

American Brown–Unlike their milder British counterparts, American browns tend to favor higher alcohol content, less malt influence, and higher hopping rates.

American Cream Ale–This is a unique American style. Cream ale is top-fermented and then aged cold like a lager. Cream ale is generally light-bodied and golden in color. Hopping rates are low, but may be detected. The recent flurry in microbrew production should prove beneficial to the integrity of this often-snubbed beer.

American IPA–Maltier, richer, and more potent than the American pale, these ales are very popular in the US. Caramel notes initially coat the palate, but are ultimately dominated by a clean bitter finish, crowned by the spiciness and floral characteristics of American-grown hops. This American interpretation is perhaps closer to the original IPA than contemporary British representatives, which tend to be sweeter and less aggressively hopped.

American Pale Ale–These ales are drier than the British style, favoring American hop qualities. The color range is from a light straw to reddish-brown.

American Wheat–Several microbreweries produce light, tart ales composed of malted barley and wheat. Some bottle-condition their beer, leaving the yeast sediment characteristic of Hefe-weizen, while others filter to a sparkling gold. Many Americans drink these ales with a slice of lemon on the rim of the glass, the nineties version of the Corona-lime craze.

American pale ale

Lager

Lager beer is cold-fermented and aged using yeast strains that tend to thrive in the bottom of the fermentation vessel. Since lager yeast converts a wider variety of malt sugars (notably, raffinose), lagers are cleaner tasting than ales.

AUSTRIA

Vienna–The famous Austrian brewer, Anton Dreher, created this lager in the mid-nineteenth century. During Austria's brief Empire in Mexico, the style gained in popularity and continues to be made in Mexico, but has since faded from the market elsewhere. It ranges in color from amber to deep copper. This beer has a medium body, with moderate notes of toasted malt on the palate, and a low to medium hop flavor and aroma.

CZECH REPUBLIC

Bohemian Pilsner–In 1842, in a small brewery in Plzeň (or Pilsen), Josef Groll created a revolutionary style of beer that has been imitated around the world ever since. Improved technology and a new understanding of the fermentation process set the stage for this major style of beer. Unlike the dark, murky ales and lagers that had preceded it, Pilsner lager shone like liquid gold in the glass. The soft waters around Plzeň perfectly matched the gentle spicy flavor and aromatics of the indigenous Saaz hop. Traditional Bohemian Pilsners are light- to medium-bodied, have a smooth malty flavor, and are balanced by Noble bittering hops.

GERMANY

Traditional Bock–Bread and beer share many characteristics, from historical beginnings to the ingredients that make the two products. Hence, beer is often referred to as "liquid bread" and this phrase may have its derivation in the abbeys of Europe. Bock is a rich malty brew that was consumed by fasting monks as a source of liquid nutrition. Bock is loaded with the sugars and carbohydrates that make up its sweet malt profile. Hops are used to balance the malt, but bitterness, flavor, and aroma are low. It may have a slight chocolate flavor, as well as some butterscotch undertones.

- **Doppelbock**–Stronger versions of the traditional bock, these lagers are full-bodied, and are pungent, sweet, and complex. Notes of fruity esters may be detectable on the nose.
- **Helles Bock**–These bocks are lighter in color than traditional bocks. However, they retain most of the characteristics of bock. The color ranges from pale to light amber. Helles Bock also lacks the chocolate character of the original.
- **Eisbock**–These are Doppelbocks, which have been cooled to freezing and removed of frozen water, resulting in a more potent brew. These taste similar to Doppelbocks, with an added warmth on the palate due to the increased alcohol.

Dortmunder–Originally brewed in the hard-water regions on the outskirts of Dortmund, this lager is full-bodied, and somewhat sweeter and less hoppy than German Pilsner (see below). This unique lager, simply called "export" in Germany, is light to gold in color.

Munich Dunkel–This is a dark, medium-bodied lager that is sweet, with notes of caramel and chocolate. Hops balance the malt but do not contribute any significant aroma or flavor.

Munich Helles–This lager was brewed in response to the popularity of Pilsners in the 1920s. While the two styles share a deep golden color, Munich Helles are maltier, and thus a bit fuller-bodied, and are less hoppy than Pilsner.

German Pilsner–This lager is brewed all over Germany and its characteristics vary slightly from brewery to brewery. Generally, these are lighter versions of the Czech Pilsner. More emphasis is placed on hops, resulting in a drier beer with a floral aroma and finish.

Rauchbier–The name means "smoke beer," which describes the resultant flavor of drying malt over an oak or beechwood fire. This is a full-bodied lager with a sweetness that lurks beneath the aggressive smoky flavor and aroma. Color is copper to dark brown, and hopping rates are low to moderate.

Schwarzbier–This dark-brown to black beer has a rough-around-the-edges malt flavor. While this medium-bodied lager provides some sweetness and chocolate flavors, these are crossed with the bitterness of added roasted malt.

Munich Helles

NORTH AMERICA

American Bock/Dark–While these are two different beers, their profiles are almost identical. Color alone differentiates these two styles, and color also distinguishes them from other American lagers. Each is light-bodied, has little or no perceivable hop aroma or flavor, and is darkened by specialty malts or the addition of caramel syrup.

American Dry–This light-bodied, effervescent lager uses genetically engineered yeast strains that break down sugars that are unfermentable by other yeast strains. American dry lager has little or no perceptible malt or hop flavor or aroma.

American Ice–This is a lager that is chilled before filtration until ice crystals form. These are removed, resulting in a beer with a slightly higher alcohol content. These beers are brewed with fewer adjuncts than most American lagers, and therefore the body is a bit heavier. Hops aroma and flavor are very low.

American Light–By law, these lagers must contain 25 percent fewer calories than standard lagers of the same brand. The body and carbonation level may be compared to seltzer water. These pale beers have no malt or hop flavor or aroma.

American Premium/Standard–Both of these pale lagers lack significant malt flavor or aroma. Hops are also low–below the threshold of perception. While American standards use a high level of adjuncts and additives, American premium typically uses fewer.

California Common Beer–"Steam" beer developed in the late 1800s in California. When the Anchor Brewing Company of San Francisco put a trademark on the term "steam," California Common was invented to circumvent infringement. These beers employ lager yeast, but ferment at ale temperatures. Where most fermentation vessels are barrel-shaped with conical bottoms, California Common is fermented in shallow, pan-shaped vessels. Further maturation at warm temperatures produces a beer that is quite different than most American lagers. Generally, these are medium-bodied, amber-colored beers, with a high hop bitterness and flavor.

Malt Liquor–Since these beers exceed legal alcohol limits to be labeled beer, the law requires that they must use this moniker.

CHAPTER TWO

How Beer is Made

An elegant marriage of ingredients

BEER IS COMPOSED OF FOUR main ingredients: malt, hops, yeast, and water. **Malt** is responsible for supplying much of the flavor, color, and texture of beer. Malt also provides a food supply for the yeast. **Hops** provide bitterness to balance the sweet sugars in the malt. The cone-shaped flower also adds aroma and flavor, and even helps to stabilize and preserve the flavor of beer. **Yeast** (used as a plural noun by many brewers, note) convert sugars from the malt into alcohol and carbon dioxide through a natural process called fermentation. **Water** is the stage on which all of the ingredients interact.

Furthermore, other ingredients may be added to achieve certain characteristics. Adjuncts (unmalted grain) and other additives can be used to augment flavor, alter color, or help make beer clearer.

These are the elements that mix, mingle, and interact to form limitless varieties of ale and lager. Armed with the proper equipment, it is the brewmaster who is responsible for the orchestration of the ingredients.

Professional brewers and homebrewers share a common goal: to make quality brew.

Professional brewing

Based out of Aberdeen, North Carolina, the Pinehurst Village Brewery is a growing company producing Scotch ale, brown ale, and golden ale.

At every level of brewing, whether at a multimillion-dollar professional operation or in your own kitchen, sanitation is a must. All tanks, lines, fittings, and filters must be free of bacteria and wild yeast.

To achieve this, the head brewer, Scott Youmans, uses caustics, heat, and Iphodor. Once the equipment is clean and sanitary, ingredients are weighed and prepared.

Grain malt must be gently cracked prior to use. This allows the internal starches, dextrins, and sugars exposure to the brew water (known as **liquor**), while keeping the husks of the grain whole and intact. The husks will later be of service. The grain is cracked in a roller mill. Two adjustable, grooved bars draw in and crack the grain. All material is collected and automatically transferred to the **mash/lauter tun** (or MLT).

▲ *The four main ingredients of beer: hops, yeast, malt, and water.*

MASHING

The mash/lauter tun is then filled with carbon-filtered water, which is heated to a temperature of 65°–67.5°C (149°–54°F), depending on the style of beer being brewed. At this point mineral salts may be added to adjust the water content. The mash/lauter tun is equipped with a rake-and-plow system, which gently stirs the grain and liquor. The mixture is then left to rest at one of the temperatures in the above range for about one hour. Care is taken to maintain a constant temperature. If the water is too hot, starch-converting enzymes within the grain will "die" (denature) and it will be impossible to use them.

During this time, starches are broken down into usable compounds. An iodine test is used to determine when starch conversion is complete. A sample from the mash/lauter tun is placed in a dimpled pan and iodine is dripped over it. If the

◄ *After the mashing, brewing salts and specialty malts are added.*

mixture turns dark purple, there are still starches present and the mashing must continue. If no color change occurs, then mashing is complete.

MASH OFF, VORLAUF, AND LAUTERING

Once starch conversion is complete, the rakes are turned off. The temperature of the mash is raised to 76°C (169°F) to denature active enzymes.

After the mash off, the head brewer begins the vorlauf. Affixed to the bottom of the mash/lauter tun is a screen. The purpose of this is to allow the flow of simple wort through a valve under the screen, while retaining the husk material. Here the husks play a vital role. By releasing some wort into a small open vessel called a **grant**, the brewer can inspect the wort for clarity. The wort is then pumped back into the MLT through a process called **vorlaufing**. The wort is circulated through the MLT into the grant and back again until two things are accomplished. First, any grain or husk material that has slipped around the screen is cleared into the grant. Second, the steady pressure of circulation causes the husks to settle at the bottom of the tank, forming a filter bed. Once this is accomplished, **lautering** may begin.

Lautering is a rinsing process. Wort is drawn from the MLT and transferred into the **brew kettle**. When the level of wort is almost down to the top of the filter bed, hot **sparge water** (60–71°C/140–60°F) is added to rinse extra sugars from the grain. Care is taken to maintain a steady flow of sparge water so as not to compact the spongy filter bed, which would restrict a steady flow into the grant and kettle. Once the kettle is filled to the proper level, the inlet valve is closed and boiling begins.

▲ *The open grant allows the brewer to visually inspect the wort for clarity.*

BOILING

The contents of the kettle are brought to a boil. A steam jacket is used as the heat source. This raises the wort to a boil, and prevents scorching by offering an even supply of heat. During the first five minutes of the boil, proteins are precipitated out of the solution. Known as the hot break, this can cause a foaming up of the wort, which, if left unwatched, could rise over the rim of the kettle, causing a boil-over. Once the wort settles down, hops are added in separate stages.

The first hops are high in bittering potential (alpha-acid resins). These are used to create a well-balanced beer. These are added early in the boil, so that the maximum amount of resin will be extracted. The second hop addition contributes some bitterness and some flavor to the brew. The final addition comes one minute before the end of the boil. These are low-alpha-acid hops, which contain oils that impart flavor and aroma.

Once the boil is completed (60–90 minutes) the steam jackets are turned off. Boiled wort contains a lot of precipitated material that would be disadvantageous to the flavor of the beer. Therefore, the clear wort must be drawn off this sediment. This is achieved by whirlpooling the wort within the kettle using internal circulation pumps. The act of whirlpooling drives the solid material (known as **trub**, pronounced "troob") into the center of the conical kettle bottom. After 20 minutes the pumps are shut off and the wort is allowed to rest for another 20 minutes. This allows the trub to settle on the bottom of the kettle. When the wort is eventually pumped out, it is from a valve that sits higher than the collected sediment, thus avoiding the removal of trub. After whirlpooling, a sample of wort is drawn off and a hydrometer reading is taken.

▲ *At the end of the boil a sample is drawn from the kettle for a specific-gravity reading.*

PITCHING YEAST

The sanitized and cooled fermentation tank is now ready for the yeast. Pinehurst Brewery uses special yeast strains for each style of beer they produce. Microbrewers are notoriously secretive about the type of yeast they use, and Pinehurst are no exception. Ale yeast can be reused up to a hundred times.

The **lees** (yeast sediment) from previous batches is collected and stored in sanitary vessels. Scott adds the yeast to the fermentation tank and seals it off. The bottom of the tank is conical–yeast sediment is easily recaptured after each fermentation.

COOLING IN

The brewery uses a heat exchanger to quickly drop the temperature of the near-boiling wort to about 15.6°C (60°F). Pinehurst has a cold-liquor tank that is supercooled to 1.5°C (35°F) by a glycol coolant system. Hot wort is passed through one end of the heat exchanger and cold water through the other. The heat exchanger transfers the heat from the wort into the cool water, raising its temperature to about 60°C (140°F). Of course, the wort and water never make contact. The wort runs through a long network of copper pipe that makes contact with parallel piping through which the cold water is pumped, quickly cooling the wort to proper temperatures through conduction.

Also, as the cooled wort enters into the fermenter, it passes through an oxygenating stone. This is a capped piece of pipe full of microscopic holes. As the wort sprays out of the holes, it picks up oxygen from the air, which at this point is vital for yeast growth and reproduction.

The wort is allowed to ferment under a carefully regulated temperature for three to eleven days, depending on the style. Scott takes hydrometer and pH readings to monitor the rate of fermentation. Once all of the sugars are fermented, the tank is crash-cooled to 0°C (32°F). The yeast sediment is collected for storage into sterile brew pails, and the fermented wort is transferred to the aging tank.

CONDITIONING

The temperature is kept at just above freezing in the aging tank. Excess yeast and tannins (a haze-forming compound) settle to the bottom of the tank over a period of two and a half weeks. Here the beer matures and mellows in flavor. Some natural carbonation forms from the continued work of suspended yeast.

FILTERING

After aging, the beer is transferred through two filters and into a holding tank. The first filter is made up of diatomaceous earth. DE is fossilized skeletons of microorganisms that were alive during the Cretaceous period. The hard, compacted fossils filter out many proteins and yeast cells. The second filter is a plate-frame filter. This is a series of flat pads that entrap still smaller microorganisms from the beer. Besides the mechanical filtration, the pads provide ionic filtration. As the beer passes through, an overall positive charge is created, which magnetically attracts and entraps negatively charged molecules.

THE HOLDING TANK

The filtered beer is kept in a vessel called the **bright-beer tank**. Carbon dioxide is forced into the tank to carbonate the beer and keep it fresh as it awaits bottling. While the beer is already somewhat carbonated when it enters the tank, Pinehurst use a carbonating stone to add extra effervescence to the brew. The beer is then either bottled or kegged.

▼ *The final stage of the process—the beer is bottled and sent off to grocery stores, restaurants, and bars.*

Homebrewing

SCOTT YOUMANS MADE AN INTERESTING observation. "In microbrewing and homebrewing the big picture is the same. The difference between the two is that, while homebrewers tend to experiment with different recipes, we have to make the same beer batch after batch. So we have to fully understand the science behind brewing and make sure that the procedure is the same for every batch."

Indeed, as homebrewers we have the advantage of experimentation. After all, we are usually making 19-liter (5-gallon) batches for personal consumption. Pinehurst brews about 4,693 liters (1,240 gallons) per batch for public sale. To stay in business, the brewery must produce quality beer that is consistent in color and taste.

Scott also noted that homebrewers replicate professional procedures on a much smaller level. Where a brewery might spend a couple of million dollars on state-of-the-art equipment, the average homebrewer can begin brewing quality beer for less than a hundred dollars.

As for consistency, well-informed homebrewers can control many aspects of the brewing process, and create beer to their specifications every time. As you read this book, you will learn how to predict how your beer will turn out, and you will gain control over your procedure using the Homebrew Charts provided.

▼ *Most brewing supply stores sell a starter kit for the novice homebrewer.*

Brewing your first batch of beer

The previous sections outlined the professional brewing process. Each aspect of homebrewing will be explored in greater detail in subsequent chapters, and advanced concepts and techniques will be introduced.

Nothing, however, whets the appetite for this type of learning more than making a tasty batch of homebrew. While the chemical processes that transpire in pot and fermenter are complex, the procedure can be relatively simple. The Sumerians made palatable potables without potholders–or even a stove–so fear not. By carefully following the instructions in this chapter, you'll produce an enjoyable, satisfying brew that would make even Ninkasi proud.

In this chapter you will learn:

- All of the basic equipment and ingredients needed for your first batch of homebrew
- How to brew an extract-based recipe
- How to fill out an Extract Homebrew Worksheet
- Basic recipe variations and tips on how to improve your brew

Ingredients

- **2.9 kg (6½ lb) unhopped amber malt extract syrup or 2.5 kg (5.5 lb) unhopped dry amber malt extract**. Dry extract is more potent than syrup (which is diluted in water) and so less is needed.
- **42.5 g (1½ oz) Northern Brewer hop pellets**. This will provide your beer with a bitterness that will balance the sweetness of your malt.
- **28.3 g (1 oz) Cascade hop pellets**. Added at the end of the boil.
- **1056 Wyeast American ale yeast or one packet of dry ale yeast**. The Wyeast is in liquid form and comes in a "slap pack." Simply rupture an inner bladder with the palm of your hand, wait until the packet swells to proper thickness (usually a day or two), and pour it into your cooled wort.
- **1 teaspoon gypsum (optional)**. Calcium sulfate hardens your brew water, magnifying the perception of bitterness.
- **70.8 g (¾ cup) corn sugar**. Used at bottling time to carbonate your beer.
- **22.7 lt (6 gal.) tap water or bottled spring water.** Expect to lose up to a 3.8 liters (1 gallon) of water during the boil. The extra water ensures you'll have 19 liters (5 gallons) of beer in the fermenter.

Equipment

As you read the following list, you may find that you have some of this equipment lying around the kitchen. An hour of rummaging may save you some money. However, you probably won't find a hydrometer tucked away in your silverware drawer (unless you are obsessively concerned with the sugar content in your grape juice). For this and other items exclusive to homebrewing, you'll need to visit your local supply store.

Valhalla to brewers of all levels, the homebrew supply shop will offer all of the ingredients and gadgetry you may ever need. Often, these shops have economically priced starter kits containing much of the equipment listed below.

- **11.3–22.7 liter (3–6 gallon) stainless-steel stockpot or enamelware canning pot**. The larger the better and, for all practical purposes, stainless steel is best.
- **Smaller saucepan**. Used for rehydrating dry yeast and liquifying priming sugar.
- **One or two long-handled stirring spoons**. Wood can be used during the boil but sanitized plastic or stainless steel must be used when the wort is cool to avoid introduction of bacteria.
- **Cloth or muslin bags**. Used to steep your hops, these are very cheap and very useful. Purchase three for your first batch.
- **Floating thermometer**. This item, included in most kits, must be able to withstand boiling temperatures. You'll use it to gauge when your wort is cool enough for pitching (adding yeast), and to make hydrometer corrections.
- **Timer**. Get one that counts backwards.
- **Measuring cup**.
- **Primary fermenter with lid and spigot**. Food-grade plastic is good for beginners and the spigot makes transferring a breeze. There are two sizes available: 19 liter (5 gallon) and 24.6 liter (6.5 gallon). You'll need the larger for a 19-liter (5-gallon) batch.
- **Airlock and drilled rubber bung**. Airlocks make high art of low tech. These small devices attach to your primary fermenter, allowing CO_2 to escape but keeping unwanted bacteria from gaining entrance. These are included in most kits.
- **Hydrometer**. Usually included in basic kits, these are used to measure sugar content before and after fermentation to gauge attenuation and alcohol content.

- **Siphon hose**. Food-grade, clear hose used to siphon beer from one container to another. This is included in most basic kits. If you buy it separately, make sure the inside diameter is 9 mm ($\frac{3}{8}$ inch) across.
- **Bottle filler**. This hard plastic device connects to your siphon hose. Beer comes out only when the spring-activated tip is pressed into the bottom of your bottle. This is another simple but ingenious device that will save you volumes of otherwise spilled beer.
- **Bottle capper**. There are hammer cappers, two-handed cappers, and bench cappers. The two-handed type is often included in basic kits and seems the best marriage of quality and price.
- **Bottle brush**. Reaches into those hard-to-reach spaces and helps to remove those hard-to-remove spots.
- **52–54 brown "non-returnable" pop-top bottles**. Light is the enemy of maturing beer, so stick with bottles that discourage its effects. Also, screw-top bottles are impossible to properly seal and are often too thin to withstand the pressures created by CO_2 during bottle conditioning. Often, your local watering hole will happily part with a few cases of empties for a couple of bucks.
- **52–54 bottle caps**. These are available at your local supply store and are often included in basic kits.
- **Chlorine bleach**. Used to sanitize your equipment. There are a number of alternatives on the market, but bleach is the cheapest and is easy to use. Quick note: never mix bleach with other household cleaners that may contain ammonia.

Steps to successful brewing

1 **Cleaning and sanitizing your equipment and work area**
2 **Carefully following recipe procedure**
3 **Keeping thorough records**

Sanitation is a must. The object is to minimize the amount of bacteria that come into contact with your wort, thus giving the yeast opportunity to ferment properly. Brewers who overlook this step are bound to eventually wind up with a batch of spoiled beer. Furthermore, they are sure to foster future bacterial infections if spotted, nicked, or gummy equipment is not promptly replaced or thoroughly cleaned and sanitized. Admittedly, this is the least enjoyable part of brewing. However, compared with the prospect of an otherwise great batch of homebrew spoiled by an avoidable infection, it is a small price to pay.

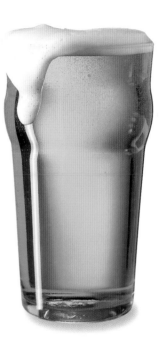

Preparation

Start to prepare at least a day in advance. If you are using a liquid yeast pack, rupture the inner bladder using the palm of your hand and knead its contents. The yeast will require a day or two to strengthen and multiply–observable as a dramatic inflating of the packet. Depending on your water source, you may want to dechlorinate your water by letting it sit in your open fermenter overnight. However, any water that is allowed prolonged exposure to air must be boiled to kill unwanted microorganisms. Since most of this water will be going into your brewpot, this is no problem.

Water reserved for direct addition into the fermenter should be either boiled in an open pot and cooled in a covered container or drawn straight from the tap or bottle. An alternative is to boil your water for about ten minutes before adding your extract. A vigorous boil will drive off most of the chlorine, and will clear "hard" water of some minerals. Next, pour most of the boiling water into another vessel–like your primary fermenter–and rinse out your brewpot to remove the precipitated minerals. Now pour your water back into the pot and you're ready to start adding your malt.

Sanitize all of your equipment, except anything metal, in a solution of 29.5 milliliters (1 ounce) of chlorine per 3.785 liters (1 gallon) of water. Allow at least a half-hour of soaking for the chlorine to do its job. Any equipment that is dirty should be first cleaned, using hot water and a small amount of detergent. Any time you use soap be sure to rinse the equipment, as any residue will discourage the heat retention of your beer. When cleaning equipment, stay away from stiff wire brushes and other abrasive scrubbing tools. These can nick and scuff plastic items, creating tiny caves for nasty microbial visitors to set up residence. Once your equipment is cleaned and sanitized, rinse it with water that has been boiled for a few minutes. Keep your sanitized equipment in a clean environment. You can use your fermenting bucket to contain smaller items, but again, use care not to damage its interior.

Next clean your work area. Scrub down your counters and stovetop, clear away any dust, and sweep and mop the floor. A final once-over with a sponge soaked in the chlorine solution will ensure that all of those kitchen creepy-crawlers are wiped away. You can minimize airborne contaminants by filling a spray bottle with the sanitizing solution and misting the area. However, make sure all of your ingredients are safely tucked away.

Brewing

Now, lay all of your ingredients out. If you're using canned malt extract syrup, you may want to place the cans in hot water to make the contents easier to pour. I don't recommend boiling them in a pot of water on the stove, as heat from the range can scorch the syrup. This will change the color of your beer, and negatively affect its flavor. Rather, fill a basin with near-boiling water, crimp a hole in each can with a can-opener, and ease them in. Ten minutes should be plenty of time to thin the viscous syrup.

1

Place the extract in hot water.

2

Add the extract to the brewpot.

3

Keep an eye on the brewpot! Use a mist bottle or adjust the temperature on your range to avoid a boil-over during the hot break.

4

Add the boiling hops.

5

Add your finishing hops five minutes before the end of the boil.

Fill your brewpot to three-quarters full of water. Bring this to a boil then remove the pot from the heat source. Open your extract and stir it in. Pour some hot water into the can to remove all of the extract. (Don't burn your hands!) Continue to stir until you are certain that all of it has dissolved. Undissolved extract will sink to the bottom, scorching when you reapply heat to the brewpot.

Now place 28.3 grams (1 ounce) of Northern Brewer hops into a hop bag and tie a knot in the top. Return your uncovered brewpot to the heat source and continue to stir. As the wort approaches boiling, chemical changes are occurring that will cause a loamy surface to form. This is called the hot break and the pot must be watched carefully. If the foam starts to rise, turn down the heat or spray clean water into the pot. The hot break can last from 5 to 15 minutes, so keep an eye on the pot until the milky surface dissolves into a dark, rolling boil.

Drop the hop bag into the pot and start your timer at 60 minutes. Stir and continue to watch the pot, as the addition of hops can cause the wort to rise again. If this happens, adjust the heat or spray clean water into the pot. At the 30-minute mark, drop in the other 14.2 grams (½ ounce) of Northern Brewer hops in the same manner you added the first addition. At the five-minute mark, add the Cascade hops in a cloth or muslin bag.

6

Cool the wort as quickly as possible, maintaining sanitary conditions.

7

Pour the cooled wort into your primary fermenter.

8

Top the fermenter off to the 19-liter (5-gallon) mark with cold, clean water.

9

Draw off a sample into your hydrometer vial.

10

Make sure you spin your hydrometer to clear away surface bubbles. This is your original-gravity reading. Drink it!

When 60 minutes are up, cover the brewpot and transfer it to a plugged-up sink basin. Fill the basin with ice water and begin your timer. Remove all hops bags using a sanitized spoon, taking care to avoid splashing. Your goal is to bring the wort from near boiling temperatures down to about 23.9°C (75°F) as quickly as possible. Wort is susceptible to bacterial growth within the range of 26.7–60°C (80–140°F). Change the sink water if it warms, or create a continuous-flow system, by drawing water out of the sink basin with a piece of siphon hose, while matching the flow with cold water from the tap. When the wort reaches about 25–28.9°C (77–84°F), it is ready for the fermenter.

Fill your fermenter with about 1.9 liters (½ gallon) of cold, clean water. Pour the contents of the brewpot into the fermenter. This is the only time that oxidation is not a concern. In fact, the introduction of oxygen is vital at this point, since the yeast will need it during the first (aerobic) stage of fermentation. Topping off your fermenter to the 19-liter (5-gallon) mark, with pre-boiled, cold water should bring your wort to pitching temperatures 23–25.5°C (74–78°F). Take a temperature reading, and place the lid loosely over the top. Draw a small amount of wort from the spigot on the fermenter and take a hydrometer reading. Be sure to spin your hydrometer in the vial to clear away any bubbles. Take the reading from the top of the meniscus (the highest level of the curved surface). If the wort temperature is above 15.6°C (60°F)–and it probably will be–you'll need to use a hydrometer correction table to get an accurate reading. The reading should be at or around 1·056. If it isn't, don't worry, different brands of extract will often supply varying amounts of sugars and carbohydrates. This reading is your **original gravity**.

Now pitch the yeast. If you are using liquid, simply snip a corner of the packet with sanitized scissors and stir in the contents. For dry yeast, rehydrate in pre-boiled, warm (32.2°C/90°F) water and cover with plastic wrap for 10 minutes. Then pour the contents into the fermenter and stir. In both cases continue to stir the wort vigorously for 5 to 10 minutes, to encourage the introduction of oxygen.

12

Stir the wort with a sanitized spoon to encourage the introduction of oxygen.

11

Pour in the prepared yeast packet.

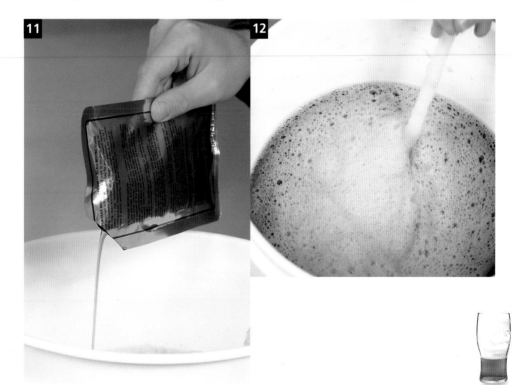

13

Tightly secure the lid on your fermenter.

14

Fill your airlock with water or vodka and wedge it in the hole of the lid of your bucket.

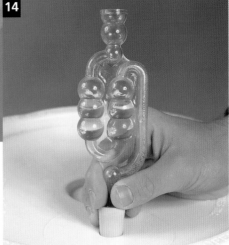

15

Pour your corn sugar into a saucepan partially filled with water. Bring the mixture to a boil.

Fill your sanitized airlock with water or high-proof vodka and wedge it into the hole on the lid of the fermenting bucket. Store your fermenter in a dark quiet place, and clean your equipment.

After a day or two you should notice bubbles plopping up through your airlock. This is good. It means that the yeast has gobbled up all available oxygen and has entered the anaerobic, alcohol- and CO_2-producing stage. This may last from four days to a week. When the bubbling has all but ceased, wait two more days, and then get ready to bottle your beer.

Use your bottle brush and some warm tap water to evict any contaminants from the interior of each bottle. Make sure any spotty or gooey deposits are completely washed out. Soak clean bottles in a solution of 29.5 milliliters (1 ounce) chlorine bleach per 3.7 liters (1 gallon) of cold water for a half hour. Rinse with pre-boiled, warm water, or simply allow it to air-dry. Immerse bottle caps in a dilute bleach solution for 20 minutes. Never boil the caps, since heat will ruin the rubber seals. Sanitize and rinse your siphon hose and bottle filler.

16

17
Pour the priming sugar into your fermenter and gently mix, taking care not to disturb any sediment on the bottom of the bucket.

16
When the sugar mixture has cooled, you can add it to your fermenter.

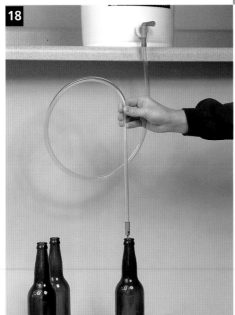

18

18
Line your bottles up and get ready to fill!

Now add your 70.8 grams (¾ cup) corn sugar into about a cup of water and stir to a boil. After 5 minutes, remove the pot from the heat. Draw some beer out of the fermenter for a **final-gravity** reading. Your hydrometer should read about 1·014. Again, if you are off by a few points, don't sweat it.

Remove the lid from the fermenter, and with a sanitized spoon gently stir in the corn sugar mixture. This added sugar will give your yeast a "boost" in the bottle, carbonating your beer.

Attach the siphon hose to the fermenter spigot and the bottle filler to the siphon hose. Gather your bottles together, get out your caps and capper and turn up your CD player. It's time to bottle!

Turn on the spigot. Now place the tip of the bottle filler in one of the bottles and press. When the beer is almost level to the rim of the bottle, remove the filler. This should give the 1.8 cm (¾ inch) space needed for proper carbonation. Any more and you'll end up with flat beer, and too much less will cause such a gaseous buildup that your bottle could explode! Place a cap over the bottle and proceed until all bottles are filled. Now crimp each bottle, mark the crown with some distinguishing letter(s),

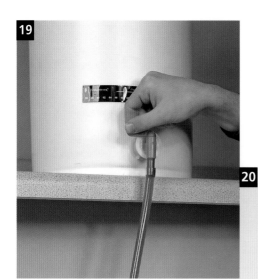

19

Turn the spigot on.

20

Place the bottle filler in a bottle, press to fill, and pull it out when the beer is near the rim.

21

Crimp each bottle and mark "First batch."

(e.g., #1 for first beer brewed), and rinse them all off. Store for two weeks in a dark place. Bottling—and kegging—will be explored in more detail later.

After two weeks, or one week for the impatient, cool down a bottle and pop the cap. You should hear a crisp hiss, the sound of excess CO_2 escaping. Slowly pour the beer into your favorite glass, being careful not to allow any sediment in. The sediment at the bottom of each bottle is normal. It's mainly composed of flocculated yeast cells and some protein and hop material. Sediment is actually rich in vitamin B12, but it will make your beer taste a little extra bitter or sharp. Try to leave it in the bottle. Enjoy!

Extract homebrew worksheets

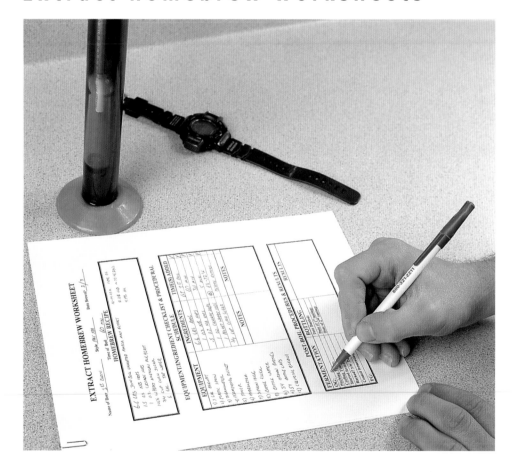

◀ *Keep thorough records to replicate a good batch, and identify and correct past mistakes.*

The Extract Homebrew Worksheets are designed to condense essential procedural information into a single, accessible page. They also serve as a journal for each batch of beer you brew. Space for data such as equipment and ingredients used, procedural information, observation notes, and a results section, allow you to plan changes for future batches and recall past homebrewing sessions. If you are trying to perfect a particular style, or are simply experimenting with different ideas, you'll have a journal that can be referenced and expanded upon.

These worksheets are easy to use, and allow any extract-based recipe to be entered. Each worksheet is divided into three sections: **Homebrew Recipe**, **Equipment/ Ingredient Checklist & Procedural Schedule**, and **Post-boil Procedures & Results**.

The first two sections will be filled out before you brew. In the Homebrew Recipe section, you are simply entering the recipe you are following. For the above recipe, you simply enter the ingredients:

Homebrew Recipe

2.9 kg (6½ lb) Amber unhopped extract syrup
42.5 g (1½ oz) Northern Brewer Hops
28.3 g (1 oz) Cascade Hops
1 packet Wyeast American ale yeast
70.8 g (¾ cup) corn sugar
22.7 lt (6 gal.) water (tap)

The next section allows you to create an equipment roster, and itemize your ingredients according to when each is added. Note that ingredient times are entered according to the total time of boil. This type of scheduling is easy to follow–you merely "check off" each addition when the correct time is reached–and it will allow greater control over your procedure as you learn more about the craft.

EQUIPMENT/INGREDIENT CHECKLIST & PROCEDURAL SCHEDULE

EQUIPMENT	INGREDIENTS	TIME(S) ADDED
1 5 gal. stainless steel pot	6½ lb extract syrup	At beginning of boil
2 plastic spoon		
3 floating thermometer		
4 fermenting bucket		
5 hydrometer	1 oz Northern Brewer Hops	At 60 minutes
6 timer	½ oz Northern Brewer Hops	At 30 minutes
7 siphon hose	1 oz Cascade Hops	At 5 minutes
8 bottle filler		
9 52 12 oz brown bottles		
10 52 bottlecaps	NOTES	NOTES
11 chlorine bleach		
12 2 new spray bottles		
13 3 muslin hop bags		
14 measuring cup		

The final section will be completed as each phase of the process is performed:

POST-BOIL PROCEDURES & RESULTS

FERMENTATION	BOTTLING	RESULTS
OG: 1·056	Date Bottled: 2/4	First beer tasted good! I'll go against my urges and wait another week before I try the next one.
Pitching Temp: 72°F	Date of 1st tasting: 2/11	
Cooling Time: 35 minutes	Date of 2nd tasting: 2/19	Second beer is excellent! Well-balanced bitterness, and the Cascade hops produce a great aroma and lingering flavor! I like the color, but there is some cloudiness. I'll see what I can do to clear this great beer up!
Started fermenting: 1/25		
Racked? y/n Days:		
Ceased fermenting: 2/1		
FG: 1·016		

◀ *This simple worksheet will help you learn how to homebrew more quickly and efficiently. As your knowledge and experience increase, so too will the quality of your brew!*

Variations on a theme

Experimenting with the basic recipe

Now that you've brewed your first batch, you know the basics of homebrewing. Consider this knowledge the basic notes of a complex musical composition. Soon, you'll be orchestrating malt, water, hops, and yeast with the finesse of a great conductor. For now, you can "riff" off your basic knowledge, changing ingredients and procedure to create several variations of the basic recipe, while gaining experience through practice.

Experiment with different ingredients. Try another brand of malt, change the style or form of hops you're using, or pitch another strain of ale yeast. Try bottled water if you used tap, or tap if you've used water from a bottle.

Use a Homebrew Chart for each recipe you create. This will strengthen your understanding of the process, and serve as a journal for each recipe.

Aging in a secondary fermenter

You can further age and clarify your homebrew by using a secondary vessel. This allows you to transfer your fermented beer off the sedimented break material and yeast, and store your beer without fear of contamination or off flavors from the trub.

The best container for this is a 19-liter (5-gallon) glass carboy. These are used commercially to store chemicals and drinking water, though the latter is quickly being replaced with plastic. You can find carboys at your local supplier, glass and china outlet stores, or, if you're lucky, at flea markets and garage sales. You'll also need a rubber stopper that fits the mouth of the carboy (no, the one you use for your plastic fermenter won't fit), and an airlock.

Once primary fermentation is complete, sanitize a length of transfer tubing. Place your primary (plastic bucket) fermenter on a table. Sanitize the carboy and place it on the floor, under the bucket. Attach the transfer tube to the spigot on your primary

▲ *A 19 liter (5-gallon) glass carboy is ideal for maturing your beer. Once the brew is siphoned off the primary sediment, you can store your beer for weeks.*

fermenter. Place the other end of the tubing in the carboy, so that it reaches all the way to the bottom. You don't want any splashing at this point, because the introduction of air will hasten oxidation. Open the valve on the spigot and gently begin to siphon. Transfer the liquid until the level in the bucket reaches the level of the spigot. Now remove the hose, attach the airlock, and store your conditioning beer in a dark, cool area.

You can also use a carboy as a primary fermenter. Many homebrewers prefer these because they are less prone to scratches and scuffs, which can harbor bacteria.

Doubtless, there will be times when you want quick ale. In a case like this you can bottle once primary fermentation has ceased. However, there are many benefits to racking your brew. First, racking to a secondary fermenter allows your beer to mature, to mellow in flavor or gain flavor from the addition of fruits or aromatic hops. Second, a couple of weeks in a secondary fermenter allows your beer to settle further. With or without the addition of clarifying agents, your homebrew will have more sparkle and less murk. Finally, beer that has been transferred off fermentation sediment can be stored for long periods of time, and bottled or kegged at your leisure. You can greatly hasten the sedimentation of yeast and other matter by "crash-cooling" your brew just after primary fermentation. Transfer your fermented beer into a secondary vessel and place it under refrigeration (about 1°C/34°F) for several days. This works especially well for beers that are going to be artificially carbonated in a keg, since much of the suspended yeast is dropped out of solution. Still, there should be enough yeast floating around for bottle conditioning. It may just take a bit longer. I first read this trick in Dave Miller's Homebrewing Guide, and later saw it in action at Pinehurst Brewery. Crash-cooling subdues yeasty flavors you may encounter in beer that matures at higher temperatures. Another way to aid in yeast sedimentation is the use of fining agents. The addition of gelatin or isinglass in the secondary fermenter will help yeast drop to the bottom of the vessel so the clear beer can be siphoned off the sediment.

▲ *You can ferment your homebrew in a carboy and substitute your airlock for a length of "blow off" tubing.*

◄ *Store your fermenting and conditioning homebrew in a dark, cool place. A plastic garbage bag keeps damaging light from messing with your beer.*

CHAPTER THREE

Ingredients

Ingredients

THE FOLLOWING SECTIONS explore the ingredients used by homebrewers in greater detail. Included in these sections are tips on how to use and store each ingredient. By understanding how each ingredient affects the characteristics of your homebrew, you will gain knowledge and control over your procedure. The end result is better beer and more consistent results.

Malt

▲ Barley is one of the earliest recorded cereals to be used for making beer.

FROM THE BEGINNING, malt has been the major ingredient in beer. Malt influences color, body, flavor, and potency. The reddish glow of an English pale ale and the silky darkness of a stout are each determined by malt. Likewise, the crisp body of a weizen and the heavy sweetness of a barley wine are each largely due to the type and amount of malt used. Malt provides fuel for yeast and is the polar partner to the bitter hop. Malt is actually the term used for grain–like wheat or barley–that has gone through the process of malting.

Barley basics

Known to botanists as *Hordeum vulgare*, barley belongs to the grass family. Barley is one of the earliest recorded cereals to be used for the making of bread and beer, dating back about 10,000 years. It is singular in its ability to thrive in extreme climates, and so is one of the most abundant crops–wild and cultivated. Though wheat has supplanted barley for breadmaking, barley is still used for the production of cereals, soups, animal feed, and, of course, beer.

Two major types of barley that are used in brewing are the **two-** and **six-row** varieties. Six-row barley has more fertile kernels per ear than the two-row type. However, the kernels on the latter are larger. Two-row barley is more commonly used as the primary grist (main malt base) in homebrewing with six-row sometimes added to supply certain other qualities.

Each kernel of barley is a seed that, if left unmolested, will drop, sprout roots, and grow into another barley plant. Like any seed it has all of the basic components needed for such a task. There is a protective covering (the husk), an internal food source (the starchy endosperm), and the infant germ itself (the embryo).

As rain is absorbed up through the plant, the kernels become heavy. The moisture-laden kernels break from their connecting axis and fall to the soil. Enzymes within each kernel are released, breaking down the starches of the endosperm into usable sugars. Soon the feeding embryo within the grain sprouts rootlets and an acrospire, rooting itself into the ground.

The malting process

The malting process is artificially controlled germination. Maltsters replicate natural phenomena by a series of **steeping** and **germination**, and then stop the process by drying the kernels through **kilning**. This procedure ensures that a good portion of the endosperm is degraded into fermentable compounds, but that the conversion is left incomplete. Just when the germination process is stopped dictates the degree to which the barley is "modified"–that is, to what degree the long-chain molecules have been broken down into carbohydrates and other amino acids. Undermodified kernels contain long-chain molecules, which are difficult to utilize, while overmodification results in a large percentage of malt sugars that would lend little complexity to beer. Well-modified malt contains enzyme-degradable materials that give body, sweetness, and alcoholic potency to beer.

Steeping of the grains takes place in a water-filled vat. The water is changed regularly to discourage microbial contamination, and one or more "air-rests" ensure that the kernels don't die from lack of oxygen. During this time, water is absorbed into the barley. When the moisture content of the kernels is about 50 percent beyond their original weight, they are ready for the germination room.

Here, the kernels are spread out on the floor and held at 15.6°C (60°F) for about four to six days. During this time, air is blown onto the kernels to promote aerobic respiration–replicating what would happen normally in the field. The grains are turned regularly to keep the sprouting shoots from becoming entangled, and to discourage decay. It is here that the hard endosperm is attacked by starch-degrading enzymes within the grain, creating shorter-chain starches and sugars that would be later consumed by the growing embryo. Once the acrospire reaches a length of about three-quarters that of the kernel, the grains are removed for drying. At this point, the modified barley is termed "green malt."

Kilning the grains is a delicately controlled drying process. Far from the fire-breathing kilns that glazed our clay pots in high-school shop class, these ovens slowly raise the temperature of the grains to about 48.9–54.4°C (120–30°F) over a period of 30 to 35 hours. This slow increase in heat preserves the enzymes needed for further starch conversion, and keeps the husks a pale color.

At this point the malt is ready to be used in brewing. Further heating is necessary to produce "specialty malts," malts that add flavor or color but cannot form the bulk of fermentable materials.

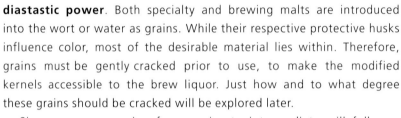

Malt forms and characteristics

There are three basic forms of malt. **Malt extract** is malt that has been mashed in a kettle and concentrated into either a syrup or powder. **Specialty malts** are malts that have been further treated in the kiln to darken the color and create various flavors. This extra roasting and toasting destroys enzymes within the kernel necessary to convert starches to sugar during the mash. Therefore, these malts are used in small amounts, along with extracts or other grains, to enhance the flavor, color, body, and head-retention of beer. Brewing malts such as **pale ale malt**, can be used for the bulk of the grist. Professional and all-grain brewers use malt grain for the same reason as extract brewers use concentrates. However, unlike extracts, malt grains must first be mashed to convert starches in the endosperm into fermentable sugars. In order for this to occur, the grain must have a healthy enzyme content, or **diastastic power**. Both specialty and brewing malts are introduced into the wort or water as grains. While their respective protective husks influence color, most of the desirable material lies within. Therefore, grains must be gently cracked prior to use, to make the modified kernels accessible to the brew liquor. Just how and to what degree these grains should be cracked will be explored later.

Since your progression from novice to intermediate will follow a path of incremental steps toward more complex procedures, we'll take a closer look at each form in the order that you'll likely be using them.

Malt extract

Malt extract is the product of professionally mashed wort that has been concentrated into either dry or syrup form. In the past the extract brewer's palette was limited by the scarcity of quality products. Today, demand has prompted the emergence of a spectrum of extracts, covering almost every conceivable style. There are light, pale, amber, dark, and wheat malt extracts available in either hopped or unhopped form. When buying any of the above, try to avoid the pre-hopped extracts. Even as a novice you should have the freedom to determine which style of hops you want to pair with your extract, and you'll have more control over the flavor of your finished brew.

Extract syrup is composed of about 20 percent water, so is not quite as potent as dry extract. Therefore, a recipe calling for 454 grams (1 pound) of dry malt extract would require a bit more liquid extract to match. Conversely, less dry extract would be needed to match a grain bill calling for 454 grams (1 pound) of liquid extract. Use an 80 percent conversion factor when making substitutions, so 1 lb DME = 1·2 lb LME and 1 lb LME = 0·8 lb DME.

Most homebrewers use extract as their primary source of malt in their brew. The reason for this is simple. Many men and women find that investing the two hours it takes to make beer using extracts beats spending all day in the garage mashing and lautering. This is not to say that extract brewing is entirely simple. Many very bad beers have been made using extract syrup. The difference between the all-grain brewer and the extract brewer is that the latter has been given a head start. Once the all-grain brewer is finished sparging, he or she is at the point that the extract brewer is when the syrup is stirred into the brewpot. From that point on, the two are on equal footing.

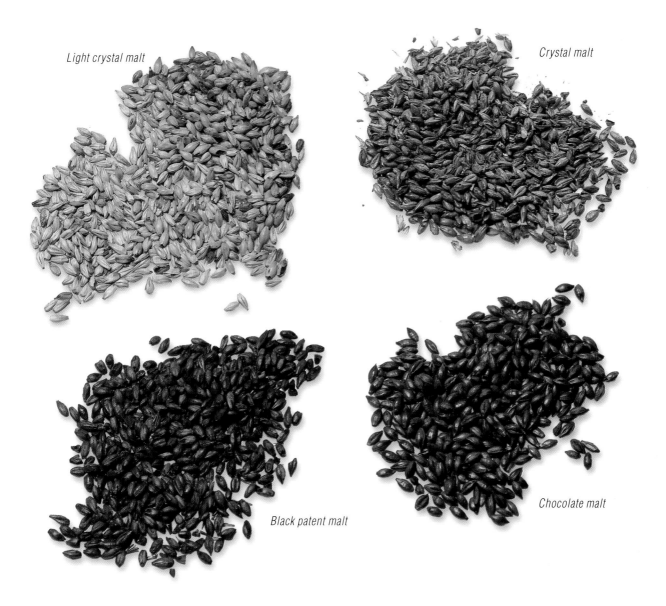

Light crystal malt

Crystal malt

Black patent malt

Chocolate malt

Specialty malt

The addition of specialty malt will greatly enhance the quality and variety of your homebrew. Moreover, it is very easy to use. With just a few extra steps, and a couple of pieces of equipment, you'll produce homebrew that is fresher-tasting, fuller-bodied, and more accurately colored to your specifications.

Crystal Malt–Sometimes called caramel malt, this is used to enhance sweetness, body, and color. Crystal malt is made by kilning undried green malt to mashing temperatures (65.6–70°C/150–58°F). This converts the starches into sugar. The malt is then kilned at higher temperatures, "crystalizing" the interior sugars into a hard glassy mass. Further kilning dictates the final color of the malt, which ranges from a light, strawlike color to a deep caramel.

Chocolate Malt–Used in darker beers, this is dried malt that has been roasted in a kiln until a dark-brown color is reached. Higher temperatures are needed to produce the chocolate color, but care is taken to maintain a smooth, uncharred flavor.

Black Patent Malt–Ever notice the sharp, coffee-like flavor of a dry stout? Then you have most likely tasted the effects of this very high-kilned malt.

Dextrin or Carapils® Malt–This light malt contributes little flavor to beer, but is used to enhance body and promote head retention.

Victory Malt–This British malt lends a toasted flavor to dark lagers and ales. Used often in brown ale and porter, the aroma is perceived as biscuit-like.

Using specialty grains

1

Heat the water to
68.3°C (155°F).

2

Put the grains into the
water and steep for
30–45 minutes. Using
a straining bag allows
for "no mess" grain
additions.

3

Gently stir to aid in
the extraction of
"goodness" from the
grains.

4

Maintain a
temperature of
65.6–70°C
(150-58°F).

The addition of specialty malt is a simple procedure. If you are using an electric range, simply add the cracked grains via a cloth or nylon grain bag (available at most supply shops) to 11.3–19 liters (3–5 gallons) of cold water. Heat the water to near boiling and scoop out the bag with tongs or a fork, and squeeze the juices back into the pot by any method except using your hands. Drape the bag over the pot and use your spoon to extract the "goodness," or use two kitchen plates held over the pot and squeezed like a vise. Now bring your water to a boil and proceed as if you were making an extract brew. For more control, and possibly a better yield, heat your water to a temperature of about 68.3°C (155°F). Steep the grains for 30–45 minutes, maintaining a temperature of 65.6–70°C (150–58°F). Next, remove the grain bag and extract the juices the same way as described above. This method will make better use of the grains, and also protect against tannic (dry, astringent) off flavors derived from grain husk that has been boiled too long. However, to maintain an even temperature, I recommend a gas burner. With flame you can regulate the temperature of your water much more accurately than with an electric coil. (See the **Equipment** chapter, page 66 for gas heating supplies.)

Grain malt

Brewer's malt, or simply, malt, is often used as the primary grist by professional breweries. Unlike specialty malts, these contain enzymes that will convert starches into sugars during the mash. The amount of enzymes in malt is often referred to as diastase. Malt with a lot of starch-converting enzymes is said to have a high diastatic power. This simply means that it contains a high degree of enzymes–namely alpha amylase and beta amylase–which will quickly degrade long chains of glucose into shorter chains in the mash.

While the all-grain brewer uses malt as the whole of his or her grist, the extract brewer can use these malts to enhance the freshness, flavor, color, and body of his or her beer. This relatively simple step will give you more control over your process, raising you to the level of intermediate brewing. Later, I'll show you how to utilize this malt, but for now, let's take a look at a few types.

Pale Malt–Pale malt comes in several varieties. **Six-Row Brewer's Malt** is said to contain a high level of starch-degrading enzymes. However, because the kernels are relatively small, the grain husk comprises a high percentage of the total malt. Since too much husk material will contribute undesirable characteristics to beer (such as haze and astringency) six-row malt is rarely used as the predominant source of grist. **Two-Row Brewer's Malt** has more viable starch per husk, but often has fewer enzymes to convert the starch. In some cases, a small quantity of six-row malt is added to larger amounts of two-row to boost diastatic power. However, most homebrewers find that the well-modified two-row malts available can produce fully attenuated brews without additional enzymes. An example of a common malt used in partial-mash brewing is **Wheat Malt**. This malt is used primarily in the production of German and Belgian ales. Often used with special yeast cultures, this light malt is combined with malted barley to produce light, thirst-quenching ales.

> **MALT TIPS**
> Avoid pre-hopped extract.
> Store unused DME in a sealed container away from heat and moisture.
> Store unused grains in an airtight plastic container.
> Malt syrup contains about 20% water. If substituting DME use 20% less of the powder.
> Never boil grains, as material in the husk will negatively affect your homebrew.
> Find and use only fresh quality malts and malt extracts.

Hops

HOPS ARE NOT ESSENTIAL to the brewing of beer. However, people who love hops *love hops*. Still, nearly six thousand years of brewing coasted along hops-free, before brewers discovered that the bitter flowers on the plant provided a pleasing balance to the sweetness of the malt that was unmatched by any additive that had been previously used.

Historians figure that people started brewing with hops in the late 800s AD. Originally, they were probably added for flavor, although it wasn't long before brewers began to notice that hops also helped stabilize and preserve beer. By the sixteenth century, the use of hops had spread throughout Europe. In 1516, Bavaria enacted the *Reinheitsgebot*, a purity law that constrained German brewers to the use of only four ingredients: barley, wheat, water, and hops (yeast was implied). Initially, not everyone embraced this newcomer.

▲ *Hops growing in the wild.*

The English regarded its use with suspicion, and Henry VIII even tried to ban the import of any hopped beer. Still, like the hardy profuseness of the plant itself, the superior qualities of this once "noxious weed" were, eventually–as Schopenhauer said of truth–proclaimed as self-evident.

Today hops are prized for the wide range of characteristics they add to beer. Certain plants are cultivated for use as bittering agents, others for aroma and flavor. Brewers label the two major groups as **boiling** or **bittering hops**, and **finishing** or **aromatic hops**, respectively. Because many hop varieties weave among the qualities of bitterness, flavor, and aroma, I'll use the terms **boiling hops** for hops added to the brewpot for thirty minutes or more, and **finishing hops** for those added at the end of the boil or later. To understand the differences between these two groups, let's discuss several aspects of this wondrously versatile plant.

Cultivation and anatomy

This tenacious vine-growing plant is dioecious, which means there are both male and female varieties, though only the female is used in brewing. Hops are of the same family as the hemp plant and, like their infamous cousin, produce dense, conelike flowers. Hops are usually planted in March or April and harvested the first week of September. While this perennial plant produces buds throughout the summer, a mature vine will offer the most valuable yields at the season's end. Once harvested, the flowers are dried and quickly packaged to discourage oxidation.

Each flower, or strobile, is composed of a number of leaflike petals called bracteole. Bracteole produce lupulin, which appear as a fine yellow powder at the base of the petal. Actually, these are tiny glands that contain the resins and oils that contribute all the desired characteristics to beer. Resins give beer bitterness, while oils impart a range of flavor and bouquet. Since high levels of the bitter resin will dominate the gentler notes afforded by the oils, the two groups are roughly differentiated by the amount of resin in the plant.

Bitter resins

Lupulin glands contain two major resins: **alpha acid**, and **beta acid**. Beta acid is almost completely insoluble at normal wort pH levels, and therefore, it contributes little flavor to the finished beer. Your main concern is with the alpha acid. Herein lies all the potential bitterness needed to produce a well-balanced homebrew. Unlike beta acids, alpha acids become soluble in solution with the addition of heat. This process, called isomerization, allows the wort to retain the bittering qualities characteristic of the resins. A minimum of 20 minutes at full boil is necessary to catalyze the resins into usable form. So-called iso-alpha acids remain–to varying degrees–in suspension throughout fermentation, storage, and, most importantly, in your glass.

▲ *Whole hops.*

AA and AAU

If you want to calculate just how much potential bitterness a particular type of hops could give your beer, you need to know how much alpha acid the plant contains. Any respectable supplier of hops will list the percentage of alpha acids (AA%) on the package. The range runs from around 3 percent (mild) to 12 percent (bitter!). Brewers calculate percentage according to the weight of the alpha resin against the weight of the whole hop flower.

Alpha Acid Units (AAU) use the alpha-acid percentage of a particular hop multiplied by the weight in ounces of the hops used, to calculate how much bittering potential is going into the brewpot. The author and homebrewer David Line devised this simple formula:

AA% x weight (oz) of hops used = AAU

Most extract-based recipes list the style and amount of hops required for that type of beer. If, however, you don't have access to the listed hop, you can substitute a variety with a similar alpha-acid percentage to ensure proper bitterness.

If your supplier has neither the type of hops called for *nor* a substitute that matches the alpha percentage your recipe requires, you can use AAUs to substitute hops of disparate AA potency.

For example, say a recipe calls for 2 oz of 7·5AA% Northern Brewer hops. The AAUs would be:

7·5% x 2 oz = 15 AAU

This means that two ounces of Northern Brewer hops will give your beer 15 AAUs. Now, say you are using Brewers Gold hops, with an alpha acid content of 8·5 percent. How many ounces do you use to produce the same amount of bitterness potential (15 AAUs)? To find out, simply reverse the formula:

$$\frac{15 \text{ AAUs}}{8.5 \text{AA}\%} = 1 \cdot 76 \text{ oz}$$

Keep in mind that AAUs predict bittering potential, not actual yield. Several factors determine how much iso-alpha acid makes its way into your glass. High-gravity beers, for example, require more hops to achieve the same balance as lighter-bodied beers. Other variants include hop form (whole, pellet, etc.), freshness, and *when* the hops are added to the wort. Many recipes call for bittering hops to be added in a couple of stages. This allows the wort to retain a maximum yield, by not becoming oversaturated with too much hops at once. Also, not all hops are the same. Different varieties will impart a wide range of flavors and aromas.

So how can you predict how bitter your final brew will taste? The quick answer is to say that you can't, exactly. Brewers use **International Bitterness Units (IBU)** as a measure of the actual bitterness in beer. 1 IBU = one part per million of isomerized alpha acid. All of the major styles of beer have IBU ranges, required to accurately represent their respective characteristics.

Several ingenious people have devised formulas to help predict IBUs–many are simple, some are staggeringly complex. In the intermediate section you'll be introduced to one method you may find useful. In the meantime, don't worry about it. Even the most sophisticated predictive methods fail to consistently foretell actual bitterness. For now, just have fun experimenting. Professional breweries achieve consistency by controlled settings, repetition, and by blending several batches until a standard is met. We homebrewers don't have the equipment and time to do this. We do, however, have the luxury of experimental indulgence. We can toss an extra ounce or two of hops in the kettle on a whim, because in the bitter end we have no one to please but ourselves.

Aromatic oils

The other qualities hops give to beer are flavor and aroma. For example, the distinctive spicy finish of a Pilsner Urquell is due, in part, to the oils found within the Saaz hop. While boiling hops balance homebrew, finishing hops crown the brew with smells and tastes that please the nose and linger on the palate. Such terms as "citrusy," "floral," and "fruity" describe the delicate virtues proffered by these hops.

Like the flavor they impart, oils are much gentler than resins and will be destroyed by an extended boil. Therefore, finishing hops are best added to the wort in the final few minutes of the boil.

Another method for adding these hops is dry hopping. This involves adding the finishing hops during the second stage of fermentation, or, if you have the equipment, directly into the keg along with the finished beer. Many homebrewers feel that this process gives their beer a fresher aroma and flavor than finishing hops that are boiled at all. As a novice, you may be using a single-fermentation system. If this is the case, forget about dry hopping for now. Hops should be added only to a secondary fermenter, and only when the yeast activity has slowed, and the alcohol content is potent enough to allow such additions without risk of contamination. Adding hops to the primary fermenter is risky and, likely, ineffective. Besides risking contamination, much of the aroma may be scrubbed away by the CO_2 released during fermentation, or trapped under a barrier of flocculated yeast cells.

If you are at a point where you are maturing your brew in a secondary fermenter, here is a simple method. Sanitize a small muslin bag by boiling it for about 20 minutes. With clean (but not soapy!) hands, put the hops in the bag and tie it off at the top. After you drop in the bag, close the fermenter and leave it alone. Since they are relatively high in acids, fresh hops

HOP TIPS

Always make sure your hops are fresh.

If you buy hops packaged in clear plastic, make sure the lupulin powder is yellow. Rusty or brown-colored powder means the hops are oxidized and worthless.

If you plan on storing hops, seal them in two airtight bags and keep them in your freezer.

Add boiling hops in stages during the boil to ensure maximum bittering yield.

Cloth or muslin bags are a cheap, efficient way to add and remove hops.

Avoid oxidation and "skunky" aromas by keeping your hops and fermenting wort away from excessive warmth and sunlight.

If you're dry hopping with plug or whole hops, try dropping a few sanitized marbles into the hop bag, for sinking weight. This will give your hops maximum exposure to the brew.

1

Sanitize a small muslin bag by boiling it for about 20 minutes.

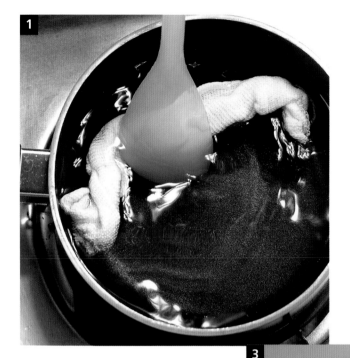

have an antiseptic quality that heavily discourages the growth of bacteria, so adding hops to maturing beer will do no harm. Sloppy practices, however, will.

All hops are unique in their own way, and each will give your beer a slightly different flavor and bouquet. Alone this can be magnificent. Working in concert, they are pure magic.

Forms and storage

Hops are available in many forms. The two most common and practical are **plug hops** and **hop pellets**. Plug hops are whole hops that have been compressed into a disk about 13 by 25 mm (½ by 1 inch). Hop pellets are machine-pulverized whole hops, formed into tiny pellets. Both of these forms have advantages over using whole hops. For one, they are easier to use and store. Since both are concentrated forms of whole hops, you don't need as much. And it's easier to store a few ounces, double bagged in your freezer, than trying to cram a bushel or two of whole hops beside your frozen yogurt.

2

Put the hops in the bag, tie off the top, and drop the bag into the secondary fermenter.

3

Once you have dropped the bag into the fermenter, close it and leave it alone!

That said, whole hops do have a valuable role in homebrewing. While it may be impractical to use them as your entire source of hops, whole hops are regarded highly for their aromatic and flavoring qualities. Pelletizing or compressing hops adulterates the composition of the plant. Some argue that such forms dilute or alter the chemical composition of the oils. Whole hops contain lupulin glands that are totally intact. As this matter is still under debate, you should feel free to experiment.

Whichever form you choose, it is essential that you store hops away from warmth and air. Hops left on the counter will begin to oxidize in as little time as a week. Fresh hops give your homebrew distinct character. Stale, oxidized hops have less to offer, and can negatively affect the flavor of your beer. Store unused hops inside two well-sealed plastic bags, and keep them in the freezer.

Yeast

AN ENGINE WITHOUT FUEL is an idle piece of machinery. Likewise, fuel is mere liquid without an engine to consume and benefit from its addition. If malt provides the fuel needed to transform wort into beer, then yeast is the engine that drives the brewing process.

Yeast consumes malt sugars, and transforms them into roughly equal parts of alcohol and carbon dioxide through a process called fermentation. Yet yeast does much more than this. Brewers count on yeast to metabolize malt sugars into alcohol. However, like the reaction that happens in the car engine, yeast produces a number of by-products. Luckily, many of these are desirable, and even define certain styles of beer. Others are less desirable, and care must be taken to minimize their effects. Different strains of yeast produce varying degrees of by-product, and this will be explored in greater detail later.

Wild and crazy guys

Yeast is a single-celled fungus that reproduces by budding, and multiplies into colonies. Thousands of species exist, adapted to almost every climate. Most species are wild, and too mutable to be relied on for the purposes of brewing. As single-celled species, they can evolve within a few generations, depending on the changing hosts and environments they thrive within. Thanks to guys like Louis Pasteur and Jacob Christian Jacobson, understanding of these fungal fermenters has led to the cultivation of the reliable yeast strains we use to this day.

The taming of the brew

The major strains of yeast available to the homebrewer are *Saccharomyces cerevesiae* (ale yeast), and *S. uvarum* (lager yeast). Though scientists consider these two strains to be basically the same, brewers distinguish the two based on how each reacts in wort. Ale yeast tend to ferment rather quickly, collecting at the top of the fermentation vessel. Slower-fermenting lager yeast seem to prefer the bottom of the vessel, and consume a greater variety and proportion of malt sugars. Alas, the brewer's distinction is based on observation, and scientists have found that both strains ferment throughout the wort, obscuring the lines a bit further. Notwithstanding, the two yeast strains require different climates to function within, and affect the potency and flavor of the final brew in different ways. Before we get into what exactly those differences are, let's take a very quick look at the fermentation process.

Fermentation

There are four major stages in the life of a wort-bound yeast cell: **lag period**, **respiration and growth**, **fermentation**, and **flocculation and sedimentation**. Once packaged yeast enters the cooled wort, it is fragile, hungry, and vulnerable. During the lag period, yeast goes to work acclimatizing itself to its new home. Enzymes are secreted that make the cell walls of the yeast permeable. Water and

---

YEAST TIPS

Buy only fresh yeast that is properly packaged and stored in a refrigerator.

Thoroughly aerate your cool wort before adding yeast.

Always maintain sanitary conditions when preparing or pitching yeast.

Store your fermenter in a dark place at temperatures consistent with the recommended range.

Primary-ferment lagers at temperatures between 65–70°F. Rack to a secondary and slowly lower the temperature to 34–48°F.

Pitch enough yeast to assure a fast and healthy fermentation.

nutrients, including oxygen, are absorbed into the cell's interior. During the second stage, the yeast strengthen and prepare to multiply. The yeast consume all available oxygen, and like most living organisms, use it for energy. Once healthy, the fungi start multiplying through a simple budding process. The oval yeast cells simply form small bumps which grow into new cells and break off. Soon, the primordial wort is swimming with hungry, healthy yeast cells, looking for oxygen to continue the respiration process.

Since the first generation already depleted the oxygen resource, the yeast exercise an anaerobic form of respiration: fermentation. Here, sugars are pillaged for energy supplies, and the yeast excrete two major by-products: ethyl alcohol and carbon dioxide. Eventually, the tiring yeast cells clump together (flocculate) and become inactive. This is the final stage of the process.

The ability of yeast to ferment sugars into alcohol is called attenuation. A typical yeast strain will convert about 70 to 75 percent of all fermentable material in the wort. Factors that influence this percentage include type of yeast used, amount pitched, amount of oxygen in the wort at pitching time, and fermentation conditions.

Ale yeast versus lager yeast

Ales have a complex, "rough-around-the-edges" quality that many people enjoy. This is largely due to the quick-fermenting ale yeast. Because it thrives in warmer temperatures, it metabolizes faster, producing more by-products than its cold-climate counterpart. Also, because it ferments a somewhat narrower scope of malt sugars, ales of similar malt content leave more body-enhancing carbohydrates than lagers do.

Ale yeast works best within a temperature range of 15.6–22.2°C (60–72°F). Excessively cool temperatures will cause the cells to go dormant, that is, to settle into a state of "hibernation." Conversely, high temperatures can result in irregular fermentation and bacterial contamination. Since ale fermentation generally takes place in the closet or basement, be careful to avoid sudden drops or rises in temperature. All yeast need stable climactic conditions. In short, don't store your fermenter near an open window or a heating duct.

Lager yeast thrives in climates of 2.24–8.8°C (34–48°F). Unless you have a time-share at a German ice cave, you'll need a refrigerator to maintain this temperature range. Lagers also require two-stage fermentation. During the first stage, fermentation is encouraged at the high end of the temperature scale, or even at ale temperatures. The beer is then transferred into a secondary fermenter (ideally a glass carboy) and allowed to continue fermenting and conditioning at gradually decreased temperatures. Obviously, this means that lagers take longer to produce than ales. While an ale may be ready within as little as two weeks, lagers require at least three weeks in the secondary. Some high-gravity lagers, such as Marzen or Oktoberfest, benefit from lagering periods of up to a year. The result of lagering is a generally cleaner-tasting, more highly attenuated beer.

Again, the distinction between ale and lager yeast activity is somewhat nebulous. As rational creatures, we tend to force neat cubes into organic polymorphous holes. As a novice, stick to quality-brand yeast that contains information relating to style and use on the package. Also, ask other brewers about the performance of specific brands and strains. Finally, experiment, experiment, experiment!

► *Dry yeast granules.*

▲ *Different forms of packaged yeast.*

Yeast forms:
dry versus liquid

Once upon a time, American homebrewers were constrained to inferior ingredients. Those who practiced civil disobedience during prohibition had to furtively assemble baking elements to concoct their fermented refreshments. Hence, the homebrewer of the 1920s was not unlike the ancient Egyptian. The stuff that made cake and bread was also used to make beer. This included baker's yeast, a viable but unreliable fermentation agent.

The legalization of homebrewing prompted higher-quality yeast, and the popularity of this hobby ensures continuation of this trend. Today, homebrewers have access to two forms of yeast: dry and liquid. Each form can be and is used to make great beer, but there are some differences in how they are used.

DRY YEAST

This form of yeast is widely used because of its ease of use. Dry yeast is simply living yeast cells that have been dehydrated into tiny granules. To ensure a level of purity and vitality, dry yeast should be fresh and completely sealed in a proper package. Yeast packets that are affixed to the bottom of pre-hopped beer "kits" are unreliable and should be avoided.

While production and packaging methods are improving, dry yeast is often slightly contaminated with wild yeast and bacteria. This is usually not a problem, because the more numerous yeast will effectively kill off its competition if it is correctly prepared and pitched. Dry yeast is commonly used for the production of ales. While there are dry lager yeast strains on the market, it is currently argued that these are essentially the same as ale yeast.

Here is a simple method for rehydrating and pitching dry yeast. Boil about 118 ml (½ cup) of water and allow it to cool to about 35°C (95°F). Sprinkle the yeast into the water and allow it to stand until it forms a mushy soup known as a slurry. Now, simply pour the slurry into the cooled wort, and with a sanitized spoon stir the wort briskly for several minutes to introduce oxygen. Cap the fermenter, affix an airlock, and store the wort at the temperature appropriate to its style. Remember to always maintain sanitary conditions when you are doing this!

Boil about 118 ml (½ cup) of water and allow it to cool to about 35°C (95°F). Sprinkle the yeast into the water.

Allow it to stand until it forms a mushy soup known as a slurry.

LIQUID YEAST

The advantage liquid yeast has over dry yeast is that it is much less likely to be contaminated, and is generally higher in quality. Liquid yeast usually comes in a "smack pack." Inside the pack is a small volume of yeast and a smaller pouch containing sterilized wort. When the pouch is broken, the yeast cells have a safe, nutritious environment in which to strengthen and multiply.

The drawbacks to this form are that the yeast are perishable and must be kept refrigerated, and that a day or two is needed for the prepared packet to become viable. There are also considerably fewer yeast cells per liquid packet than dry packet. Some homebrewers compensate by using two liquid packets, or creating a yeast starter (see Chapter Six). It is my opinion that one packet is sufficient for low- to medium-gravity worts, if the wort is sufficiently aerated. For higher gravities (>1·060) the above adjustments are a good way to ensure your yeast completes a full and healthy fermentation.

Prepare the liquid yeast packet a day or two before you plan to brew. With the palm of your hand, rupture the inside packet and knead the contents. Store the pack in an area away from excessive heat and light at temperatures between 23.3–26.7°C (74–80°F).

At pitching, maintain sanitary conditions. This is crucial when using liquid yeast, because the yeast population will be small at the outset, and vulnerable to bacterial competition. Thoroughly aerate the wort. The introduction of oxygen to the cooled wort is absolutely crucial for a healthy fermentation. With sanitized scissors, snip a corner of the packet and pour in the contents. Quickly cap the fermenter and store it in a dark environment at temperatures recommended on the label of the packet.

Water

BEER IS ABOUT 90 to 95 percent water. In its purest form, water is simply composed of two hydrogen atoms bonded to a single oxygen atom. However, this vital element, which runs underground, flows over the land, covers most of the earth, and courses through our bodies, is filled with varying amounts of mineral and organic matter. Normal drinking water is treated to eliminate most organic compounds, and to regulate the amount of minerals drawn from the raw source. Depending on geographical locale and method of treatment, your water may range from soft to hard. Besides heating and filtration, water treatment plants often add a little chlorine to ensure that the water from your tap is safe to drink (i.e. sanitary). Tap water that smells and tastes good is fine for the purposes of malt-extract brewing. Professional brewers and homebrewers who use grains tend to be more concerned with what minerals are in their water source. Why?

A closer look at water

While pure water is chemically expressed as H_2O, most water contains dissolved minerals. This is because H_2O has a slight positive and negative electrical charge, and therefore attracts mineral compounds with similar electric charges. For example, table salt (NaCL, or sodium chloride) dissolves in water because each ion in the mineral compound has an electrical charge that corresponds with the positive and negative charges of H_2O.

Certain dissolved minerals or "salts" aid in the brewing process in a number of ways. Some help make brew liquor more acidic, which is needed for malt starch conversion during the mash. Others help break down ingredients that would otherwise fall out of solution and, therefore, contribute nothing to the final brew. Still others enhance aroma and flavor characteristics proffered by the ingredients, or contribute perceptible qualities of their own.

Only specially treated water is free of mineral ions. All naturally drawn water contains varying amounts of ions, depending on geographical locale and method of treatment. Indeed, these differences dictate the style and characteristics of beer produced around the world. It's no accident that pale ale was perfected at English breweries that drew their waters from Burton upon Trent. The source is naturally rich in calcium sulfate (gypsum), which influences hop isomerization and enhances bitterness perception, resulting in a firm, dry beer. The low mineral content of the waters in the Czech Republic helped the Pilsner lager obtain its world-famous soft, rounded flavor and distinctive hop aroma. Clearly, when the professional brewer wishes to replicate a famous style of beer, he or she is very concerned with the chemistry of the brewing liquor.

Water and the malt-extract brewer

As an extract brewer, you needn't be overly concerned with your water. Malt extract is a professionally mashed wort that contains proper mineral levels. You are beginning at a stage after most of the ions have done their work, and quality beer can be produced using good, clean water. Still, certain salts can be added to the wort

to aid in various ways. We'll explore these additions in a minute, but first, what is meant by "good clean water"?

There are three main considerations the novice brewer should understand when choosing brew water:

1 **The water is safe for human consumption**
2 **The water is free from a heavy iron or metallic flavor**
3 **The water is free of chlorine aromas or flavors**

Tap water must be safe, i.e. free of pathogens and other microorganisms. Water plants use sophisticated filtering techniques to rid water of most organic material. Chlorine is often added to further ensure potability and to keep microscopic bugs from entering the water after it has left the plant. The low levels at which it is added mean it is safe for humans but toxic to microbes. However, if your water smells or tastes of chlorine, measures should be taken to remove it, as it could negatively affect the flavor and head-retention of your homebrew. This is easily accomplished by either letting the brew water stand in an open bucket for 24 hours, or boiling the water for 10 minutes prior to the addition of the extract. Activated carbon water filters are becoming increasingly popular and less expensive. Some filters attach directly to your kitchen faucet, while others are built in to pitchers. A carbon filter will rid your water of most traces of chlorine and chlorine compounds.

If your water has a heavy iron or metallic flavor, it is probably the result of old or rusty pipes in your tap system. If this is the case, use bottled drinking water, which can be purchased cheaply at the grocery store.

Keep in mind that your water can be contaminated during the brewing process. Proper sanitation of all materials that come into contact with the wort is a must. This is extremely important to remember once your kettle leaves the heat source. Cooled wort and water additions to the fermenter must be kept as sanitary as possible.

Popular brewing salts

Even as an extract brewer, you can enhance certain characteristics of your brew with the addition of certain salts. The following are cheap, accessible additives that you can add to your extract wort.

- **Gypsum** (calcium sulfate)–Half to one teaspoon of gypsum per 19 liters (5 gallons) of brew will aid in clarification, and will sharpen the perceived bitterness of your beer. Gypsum is recommended for IPAs, pale ales, and stouts. It is less often used in lager brewing.
- **Table salt** (sodium chloride)–Small additions can accentuate perceived flavors from other ingredients and give your brew a soft rounded flavor. Table salt should be used sparingly (½ tsp or less) and probably should not be used in conjunction with gypsum at the novice level. Excess levels of sodium and sulfate can cause an unpleasant harshness, quite unlike the bitterness of a well-balanced brew.

For now, as long as your water source is safe and tastes good, let water be the least of your concerns. Concentrate instead on using fresh ingredients, practicing proper technique, and thoroughly cleaning and sanitizing all equipment prior to use.

Adjuncts and other additives

ANYONE WHO HOLDS sacred the German purity law of 1516, should probably skip this section. Here you will find oats, rye, brown sugar, invert sugar, and unmalted grains—enough stuff to make the Elector of Bavaria shudder in his grave. Many American microbreweries hold their adherence to the Reinheitsgebot like a flag; after all, aren't adjuncts and additives cheap things that large breweries put in their bland beer?

This logic is reasonable. If small-scale brewing is a reaction to the high-adjunct, banal brews that have monopolized the market for so long, then quality beer should consist of only the old, time-honored ingredients. While this thought may seem liberating, it is also limiting.

Remember that you are the artist and beer is your work in progress. You have access to a limitless array of ingredients. My advice is to experiment and have fun.

Adjuncts

This is a term for any unmalted grain that is added to the brewpot to enhance color, flavor, and body (mouth-feel). Any of these grains can be added to the mash, but many are first treated to make them easier to use. Hence, you may find oat or rye flakes lining the shelves of your local supply shop. Flakes are heated and pressed grains that can be added to your wort in much the same manner as specialty grains. Other adjuncts include corn, rice, and unmalted barley.

One problem homebrewers frequently come across when using flaked grains is a thickening of the wort. To avoid this, keep your additions relatively small, and steep them in as much water as your pot can safely hold (remember—leave some headspace for the boil!).

▶ *Many adjuncts, like wheat, come in many forms. This is torrified wheat and flaked wheat.*

Sugars

While mashing converts complex carbohydrates into various sugars, many types of sugar can be added directly to the wort. Corn sugar (glucose) is often used for priming homebrew. This simple sugar is completely fermentable, and will boost the potency of your beer. It will also, however, produce a thin, cidery brew if used in any great quantity. Corn sugar is like nitroglycerin. A small amount before bottling will get your yeast pumping, but too much at any time will prove unreliable and potentially explosive in the bottle.

Some sugars are necessary for the accurate replication of a particular style. Many Trappist brews contain invert and/or candi sugar to add potency and flavor without added body. Other sugar products include treacle, molasses, caramel, and beet sugar. While each of these sugars contributes its own unique qualities to various styles of beer, you should keep experimental levels low until you know exactly how each will react in your homebrew.

Fruits and spices

These are used to add additional flavor to homebrew. Fruits such as cherries, raspberries, peaches, blueberries, and apricots can be used as supplements to many styles of brew. Extracts are often available at homebrew supply shops or can be purchased via mail order. Fresh fruit can also be used, but care must be taken to avoid off flavors. Freezing fresh fruit, or heating it to 48.9°C (120°F) for 20 minutes, will minimize microbes. If you heat your fruit be sure to maintain the above temperature. Excessive heat will extract pectin from the fruit, causing unpleasant flavors. Add fruit to a secondary fermenter only when yeast activity has slowed. Buckets are ideal for fruit additions, since they allow more headspace for the sugary produce to churn

▲ *Add fruit to the secondary fermenter in a fine-mesh nylon steeping bag.*

◄ *Fruits such as peaches, raspberries, and blueberries can be used to flavor your homebrew.*

and foam. Also, fine-mesh nylon steeping bags will hold your fruit in one place, making siphoning easier. After two weeks, rack the mixture, without the fruit chunks, into a carboy.

Spices such as cinnamon, coriander, spruce, licorice–the list goes on and on–can be added to your homebrew. Generally small amounts of these can be added during the final 15 minutes of your boil. Use spices with care, and always add in small additions until you understand how each affects the flavor of your final homebrew.

Finings/Clarifiers

The following products can be added to your homebrew to aid in clarification. Most work by adhering to such haze-causing substances as suspended proteins, yeast, and carbohydrates, and dropping them to the bottom of the brewpot, fermenter, bottle, or keg.

- **Irish Moss**–This is actually a form of seaweed whose active ingredient, carrageenan, is a negatively charged substance that attracts, and drops from suspension, positively charged proteins. Irish moss is used to prevent "chill haze," which is largely composed of such excess proteins. One teaspoon added during the last 15 minutes of the boil will help clear your beer.
  - **Isinglass**–This is a palatable term for pulverized fish swim bladders. This fining agent aids in clarification by settling suspended yeast during aging in a secondary fermenter. Don't add during primary fermentation.
    - **Gelatin**–This is added before bottling to settle suspended yeast and protein matter.
    - **Polyclar**–This polymer traps suspended proteins in the wort and drops them from suspension. Add a few hours before bottling.

▶ *Additives, like Irish Moss, help clarify the brew.*

CHAPTER FOUR

Equipment

Equipment

◀ *Equipment for a more complete system.*

THE POPULARITY OF homebrewing has prompted the emergence of a cornucopia of brewing equipment and gadgetry. What was once a grass-roots venture where "equipment" meant a pot, a bucket, and a couple of dozen bottles has proliferated into a national hobby supported by businesses that supply everything needed to brew professional-quality beer, along with some technocrat extravagances.

This chapter lists and describes all of the equipment you'll need to brew extract and partial-mash beer. The accessories you'll need to bottle and keg your homebrew are also covered. By this point, you may have acquired a basic kit that has gotten you through a few batches. These "essentials" are detailed here, along with other items that you'll want to upgrade your homebrewing system.

▼ *Brewpot*

Pots and pans

Brewpots

Brewpots come in a number of sizes and forms. While the novice might need only an 11.4 or 15.1-liter (3- or 4-gallon) saucepan, the intermediate and all-grain brewers require vessels that can accommodate larger volumes of wort. Some of the more popular types used are made of stainless steel, enamelware, and copper. Many advanced brewers convert commercial kegs into brewpots. This allows the brewer a large, durable vessel that can hold 19 or 38 liters (5 or 10 gallons) of wort. These can be purchased through mail-order companies, or, if you're handy with tools, modified at home.

For performance and affordability, you can't beat stainless steel. It is durable, conductive, and easy to clean. A large saucepan is sufficient for extract brewing. As long as you can boil at least 11.3 liters (3 gallons) of wort and retain a few inches of headspace to guard against boil-overs, you're fine.

As you progress into such intermediate steps as partial-mashing and calculated hop scheduling, you'll want to buy a larger pot. These can be found at the local homebrew store or at a restaurant supply shop. All-grain brewers often use kettles large enough to accommodate 22.7 liters (6 gallons) of wort, which will eventually be boiled down to a 19-liter (5-gallon) batch. For the novice and intermediate brewer, this is unnecessary.

A 19- to 26.5-liter (5- to 7-gallon) stainless-steel pot is practical for the partial-mash brewer. A second, smaller saucepan can be used for the steeping or mashing of any grains that may be added.

▶ *Funnels*

Strainers, funnels, and spoons

A large metal strainer is useful during a few stages of the homebrewing process. For one, it is an easy way to withhold hop and trub matter when pouring your chilled wort into a fermenter. For the partial-mash brewer, it can be used for sparging grains into the brewpot.

Funnels can be used for pouring cooled wort and yeast slurry into the narrow neck of a carboy. A sanitizable plastic funnel is sufficient and stainless steel is even better.

A couple of long-handled, sanitizable spoons will prove invaluable. You'll use your spoon to gently stir the boiling wort, to agitate the cooled wort after the yeast is pitched, and to extract such items as the grain and hop bag, and your floating thermometer.

The best spoons for brewing are either stainless steel or food-grade plastic. Wood is not suitable for stirring cooled wort, because it is porous and cannot be sanitized.

▲ *Spoons*

Fermenting equipment

▲ *Plastic fermenting bucket.*

Plastic buckets

If you want to use plastic then go for the buckets sold at the homebrew shop. These are food-grade and have a rubber ring in the lid that assures a tight seal. Also, these buckets have a pre-drilled hole in the lid to accept an airlock, and some have a spigot near the base for easy transferring and bottling.

These vessels are great for single-stage fermentation. The large opening in the top makes pouring the chilled wort from the brewpot easy, and built-in handles make for simple transport from kitchen to storage.

Plastic is not generally recommended for extended fermentation. Even food-grade plastic contains microscopic holes that tiny microbes can eventually find their way through. For lagering, glass is ideal.

Plastic is easily scuffed. This creates niches that can harbor bacteria. Old, stained, and scuffed plastic fermenters should be replaced, or substituted with glass carboys.

Plastic or glass: which is better?

Plastic fermentation buckets make fine vessels for quick-fermenting ales, or as primary fermenters. However, because of their slightly porous structure, fermenting beer should not be stored in plastic for more than two or three weeks. Glass carboys are superior for long conditioning times and for lagering. Many homebrewers primary-ferment in plastic and condition in glass. Since most buckets have plastic spouts near the bottom of the vessel, liquid is easily transferred to a carboy. Assuming a good cold break and yeast flocculation, most sediment will be left behind during transfer, because of the slightly elevated placement of the tap.

Carboys

These are glass containers commonly used for storing water and chemicals. Carboys are ideal for second-stage fermentation, or maturation. They are generally obtainable in either 19- or 24.5-liter (5- and 6½-gallon) sizes. For ales, you can primary-ferment in a bucket and transfer your wort off the accumulated sediment into a 19-liter (5-gallon) carboy for extended maturation. For primary fermentation, the larger size carboy is recommended.

As long as your carboy is properly sealed with either an airlock or blow-off tube, you can let your beer age for as long as you like. Glass has an impermeable molecular bond, so you don't have to worry about intrusive microbial contamination. This is particularly important in lager brewing, where slow fermentation in a second vessel can require weeks or months.

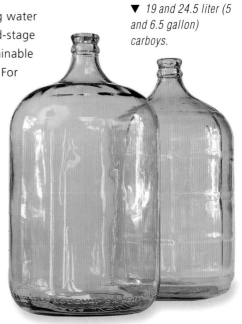

▼ *19 and 24.5 liter (5 and 6.5 gallon) carboys.*

Glass, however, is fragile. Carboys are not built to withstand very hot temperatures, and will break if you pour near-boiling wort into an empty vessel. When transferring wort into a carboy make sure that either the wort is cooler than 37.8°C (100°F) or there is some cold water in the fermenter to absorb the heat shock.

They also tend to be a bit unwieldy. Be careful when moving a full, heavy carboy. And make sure it is completely dry. Heavy, unwieldy, and slick make for a potential disaster. At the very least, you'll lose the beer you worked so diligently to craft. You can buy handles that fit around the neck of the carboy for easier transport. Ask your shop owner about his or her experience with these as to how effective they are.

Carboys are also harder to clean and transfer wort from than their plastic counterparts. Always fill your carboy with water immediately after use, to loosen any sediment that collects on the bottom and sides. Carboy brushes and bottle-washers, listed below, are great ways to scour the scourge from your carboy.

Transferring wort to a secondary fermenter, or to bottles or a keg, requires the use of tubing, the size and specifications of which are listed below.

Some companies have devised special stands that allow you to invert your carboy during fermentation. This would seem to have several advantages. First, gravity will make transferring a breeze. Second, you can remove all sediment that has collected around the neck. Finally, you can recapture flocculated yeast cells for future use. Check around.

▲ *Airlocks and rubber stoppers fit into the lid of your bucket or the mouth of your carboy. During fermentation, CO_2 is released. Airlocks allow this gas to escape while protecting your beer against outside elements.*

Tubing
BLOW-OFF

This is heavy-duty food-grade tubing that has an outside diameter of about 3.1 cm (1 ¼ inch). This can replace the airlock on your carboy. By stuffing one sanitized end into the filled, cool carboy and the other end into a bucket of weak bleach/water solution, you have a seal that is secure.

Blow-off tubing is recommended if you are using a 19-liter (5-gallon) carboy for primary fermentation, or expect a vigorous fermentation. The advantage here is that some of the early, undesirable compounds produced during fermentation may be expelled into the bucket. Also, airlocks can pop off carboys due to the excess pressure of escaping gases during primary fermentation. This is not really a concern if you are using a plastic bucket.

▲ *Blow-off tube.*

TRANSFER

This is cheap, easily obtainable, and essential in all levels of brewing. The best place to find the proper-size tubing 9 mm (⅜ inch) outside diameter, 8 mm (⁵⁄₁₆ inch) inside diameter, is at your local homebrew supply shop. I recommend purchasing 1.8-meter (6-foot) and 90 cm (3-foot) lengths.

The longer piece can be used for transfer from one vessel to another and for bottling from a carboy. The shorter one can be directly attached to your plastic fermenter spigot for bottling.

As with all equipment, keep your tubing clean, and sanitize it before use. If it's old, scuffed, or permanently stained, buy more. It's a worthwhile couple of dollars spent.

Measuring devices

Thermometers

The extract brewer will use a thermometer to determine when the wort is cool enough for pitching. The thermometer takes on more importance with the addition of specialty and mashing grains. Since it is important to keep a certain temperature range during the steeping of grains, you'll want a thermometer that can be kept in the pot for frequent readings. A thermometer used in brewing must be able to withstand boiling temperatures.

Meat and dairy thermometers are both useful. Usually, you can pick up a floating thermometer at any homebrew shop. These are nice, because they can be left in the pot throughout the entire brewing process, eliminating the need for resanitation.

Many supply shops sell stickers that can be affixed to your fermenter. By checking this "thermometer" now and again, you can make necessary adjustments to raise or lower the wort temperature during fermentation.

▲ *Different kinds of thermometers are available to use for homebrewing.*

Triple-scale hydrometer

This device is used to measure attenuation, or the degree to which the yeast converts wort sugars into alcohol. This is helpful in gauging when fermentation has ceased. If the hydrometer reads the same number two days in a row, primary fermentation is complete. Hydrometers read in three scales: specific gravity, degrees Plato, and alcohol percentage. The most commonly used and referred-to scale by American micro- and homebrewers is specific gravity. Hydrometers measure the density of a liquid against the density of water. A hydrometer immersed in water at 15.6°C (60°F) will read 1·000 specific gravity. Any solids added to the water will increase its density, causing the hydrometer to rise in the solution and display a higher number. Obviously, wort is denser than water. Alcohol, on the other hand, is lighter than wort. During fermentation, as the yeast convert sugars in the wort into alcohol, the density will drop. Therefore, the first reading (original gravity) will be higher than the last reading (final gravity).

The Plato scale measures the amount of sucrose by weight in a solution. While there are many sugars in wort, sucrose provides the highest increase in specific gravity. This scale measures the amount of sucrose conversion during fermentation.

You can also gauge the potency of your brew by taking an initial and final reading of the alcohol scale. Simply subtract the final number from the original, and you've got the alcohol by weight.

A vial and stand can be purchased at most supply shops for use with the hydrometer.

▲ *A wine thief or turkey baster can be used to extract wort from your carboy fermenter so you can take a hydrometer reading. They must be cleaned and sanitized.*

MEASURING CUP/SCALE

Both of these are used to measure the addition of ingredients. The scale can be used to measure the weight of added hops and other ingredients, and the measuring cup can be used for the addition of priming sugar. Of the two, the measuring cup is more useful. Most homebrew shops have scales on the premises, and ingredients are often packaged in convenient sizes.

Wort chillers and other cool stuff

Immersion wort chillers

An immersion wort chiller is a 6–9-meter (20–30-foot) length of copper tubing that is coiled into a stack. The chiller is placed in the wort and cold water is pumped through the copper tubing, cooling the beer. This can bring 19 liters (5 gallons) of near-boiling wort down to pitching temperatures in 15–20 minutes. While immersion wort chillers should be regularly cleaned, you can sanitize yours easily by placing it in the brewpot for the last 20 minutes of the boil. Incidentally, the trace copper ions that will end up in your brew act as yeast nutrients.

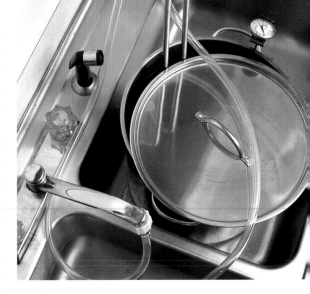

◀ *Add the wort chiller to the wort 15–20 minutes before the end of the boil to sanitize it.*

Counterflow wort chillers

Counterflow wort chillers are more expensive and require more attention. These are constructed of 4.5–6 meters (15–20 feet) of copper tubing inside rubber tubing of a slightly shorter length. Helped by a few attachments, the hot wort passes through the copper tubing as cold water is pumped through in the opposite direction, rapidly chilling the wort. The copper must be sanitized after each use by pumping through boiling water. If cared for properly, the counterflow system is superior to the immersion chiller. First of all, counterflow chillers cool the wort in a closed environment. This means that your wort is insulated against airborne bacteria and wild yeast. Counterflow chillers also cool the wort faster than immersion chillers.

Experiment with a number of techniques before making any large investments. Some homebrewers find that simply placing the brewpot in a sink filled with ice water, or creating a siphon-system as illustrated in Chapter Three, is sufficient for cooling purposes. Start with simple methods and log the efficacy of your system. Record how long it takes to cool your wort to pitching temperatures. Also, note any possible avenues for contamination that your system allows. Work your way up from simple to complex, slowly.

▲ *Using a wort chiller accelerates the cooling down process.*

Refrigerator

A spare refrigerator is almost a necessity for lagering beer. It can also be converted into a kegging system. Hunt down used refrigerators at garage sales or in the classified ads.

Gas burners and other hot items

AT SOME POINT, you may find that the electric range on your kitchen stove just isn't doing the trick. Flame boils water faster, and it is easier to maintain consistent temperatures. Even if you have a gas burner range, you'll probably notice that it won't heat large volumes of wort to boiling temperatures very quickly. Kitchen ranges also don't accommodate large brewpots very well. Luckily there is an option. Take it outdoors!

Outdoor propane cookers

These are freestanding steel burners that connect to an ordinary propane tank (like the one used for gas grills) via heavy-duty tubing. These relatively inexpensive devices will accommodate large vessels, and put out a lot of heat. Most will bring 19 liters (5 gallons) of water to a full boil in 10 minutes. Just as you wouldn't dream of bringing your gas grill into the kitchen, don't even consider using a gas burner indoors. Propane is a toxic, highly flammable gas, and should be used only in a well-ventilated area such as a back porch or garage with the door open. Always make sure all fittings are secure, and check for leaks by rubbing a little soapy water around suspect areas. If you see any bubbling, you've got a leak.

▶ *Gas burner and propane tank.*

Ingredient accessories

▲ *Muslin and grain-steeping bags.*

Steeping bags

Many brewers steep their cracked specialty grains in the main brewpot prior to the introduction of malt extract. For this, there are nylon and cloth bags widely available at most supply shops.

For no-mess hop additions, you can use cloth or muslin bags. These are very cheap and effective.

Storage containers

If you want to store a little extra grain for your next batch, try using a Tupperware container that best accommodates the amount of surplus grain. Store in a cool dry area, since moisture and exposure to air will encourage all manner of microbial and possibly even visible critter infestation.

Hops can be stored in two sealable plastic bags in the freezer for a few months. Just make sure all the air is squeezed out and the bags are tightly sealed.

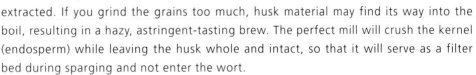

Grain mills

Any grains added to the wort must be gently cracked prior to use. This exposes the modified kernel to the heated water, which will absorb and convert the sugars and starches therein. There is a degree of specificity involved in this procedure. If you don't crack the grain husks enough, little "goodness" will be extracted. If you grind the grains too much, husk material may find its way into the boil, resulting in a hazy, astringent-tasting brew. The perfect mill will crush the kernel (endosperm) while leaving the husk whole and intact, so that it will serve as a filter bed during sparging and not enter the wort.

Some supply shops sell pre-crushed grains or have grain mills on the premises. If you want to use the latter, be sure that all the debris is cleared out of the mill. You don't want the powdery remains of someone else's grain in your bag. The alternative

is to purchase your own grain mill. While this is more of a concern for all-grain brewers who use large amounts of malt, the specialty and partial-mash malt-extract brewer may find these devices helpful. There are several models on the market.

Coffee grinders can be used, with some success, by extract-brewers who wish to add small amounts of specialty grain. Keep in mind, however, that the primary function of these devices is to grind coffee grains. Therefore, they can't be relied upon to crack barley with any consistency. Often, a good portion of the husk is pulverized along with the endosperm. If you have a coffee grinder at home, try using it only for specialty grain additions. Place the grains in a grain bag to minimize the addition of husk material.

The Corona Mill has long been a staple in the all-grain brewer's arsenal. This is a simple, hand-cranked unit that is definitely a step up from the coffee grinder. The Corona Mill was originally designed to grind corn, although it can be adjusted to accept barley. Some all-grain brewers have devised systems that allow the use of a hand-held drill to replace the manual crank, and have constructed add-on boxes that allow a greater amount of malt to be fed into the grinder at once.

Homebrewing roller mills attempt to replicate professional mills to varying degrees of success. Unlike the grinding action of the above tools, roller mills utilize rollers made of cold-rolled steel to draw in and burst the malt. This leaves the husk intact while crushing the endosperm.

When considering the above, my advice is to start cheap and work your way up. There is no reason why you should spend a lot of money on a top-notch roller mill if you're simply adding some specialty grains to your wort. Try purchasing pre-crushed grains, or use the homebrew supply shop mill, if yours has one. Again, concentrate on technique. Once you are confident that your procedures are sound, then start shopping around for more expensive equipment.

◄ *The Corona Grain Mill, a useful gadget for the homebrewer.*

Filtering and sanitizing equipment

Water filters

All municipal water is treated with some level of chlorine. While an excess of this chemical will give your water a "swimming pool" taste, a certain amount is needed to keep the water source sanitary. If you can smell and taste the chlorine in your water, chances are you'll smell and taste it in your beer. In Chapter Three, two methods were offered for dechlorinating your brew water: allowing your water to stand overnight in an open container, and pre-boiling your brew water for 10 minutes before adding any ingredients. Each of these procedures will eliminate most of the chlorine in your water.

An easier and more effective method is to employ a charcoal (carbon) filter. These connect right to your tap and eliminate all traces of chlorine and chlorine compounds. A high-quality filter may seem a little expensive, but will last a long time. If you find that you are resorting to bottled water for every batch because you can't get rid of the chlorine taste in your water, consider investing in a filter.

Beer filters

As a nation bred on straw-colored transparent beer, Americans are obsessed with beer clarity. Some people even argue that any cloudiness is the sign of inferior brew. There is some truth in this. Certain bacterial infections can cause strange-looking beers (the corresponding tastes are even stranger), and an excess of suspended proteins and sugars can cast a haze over your chilled homebrew. Still, for many styles of beer–for example, many wheat ales–a little cloudiness is expected. When you consider the thin homogeneous beer we often use as the standard, it should be clear that clarity doesn't necessarily equal superior brew.

▲ *Different types of water filter.*

For those who want to rid their beer of haze, there are filters that will remove the responsible materials. Two popular types of filters are cartridge and plate filters. Both require a CO_2 tank to force the beer through tiny holes that trap yeast, bacteria, and protein-tannin molecules. There are inserts for each of these filters that provide various degrees of filtration. The pores range from 5–0·5 microns in diameter. Considering that one micron is one-thousandth of a millimeter, you can imagine how small these pores are.

On a microscopic level, yeast are the big fish in the sea. Consequently, they are often the first to be caught in the tiny net of filtration. However, you need yeast in your bottle if you want to achieve carbonation through conditioning. There are systems that allow you to artificially carbonate bottled beer, but this complicates matters further.

Filters work best with kegged beer, which can be easily carbonated by forcing gas into solution via a CO_2 tank.

Cleaners and sanitizers

There is a difference between cleaning and sanitizing. You can't sanitize equipment that you haven't yet cleaned, and clean equipment cannot be used until it is sanitized. Clean equipment is well scrubbed and free of any spots, stains, and residues. Since bacteria can establish thriving communities in the smallest bits of residue, these must be eliminated before you take measures to evict any rogue microbes. Sanitation is not the same as sterilization. A sterile environment is impossible to achieve, except under confined laboratory settings. Sterilization is both impractical and unnecessary for the homebrewer. Sanitation is the removal of most harmful bacteria and wild yeast, and can be easily achieved with the proper tools and chemicals. The following is a list of such items.

BOTTLE BRUSH/CARBOY BRUSH

These are used with water and cleaning/sanitizing compounds to loosen and remove stuck-on residues. Swishing water in your mouth won't remove stubborn particles; likewise spraying and soaking bottles and carboys won't rid the containers of accumulated sediments. In both cases a stiff-bristled brush will wipe those deposits away. Carboy brushes are longer than bottle brushes, and are often bent at an angle so you can scrub the inside of the neck.

▼ *Bottle trees are perfect for drying sanitized bottles.*

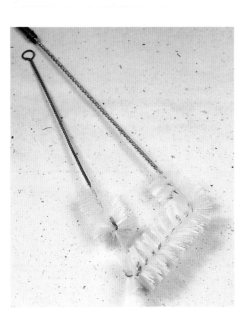

▲ *Carboy and bottle brushes.*

cleaners/sanitizers

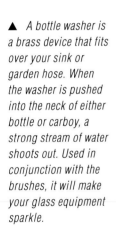

▲ *A bottle washer is a brass device that fits over your sink or garden hose. When the washer is pushed into the neck of either bottle or carboy, a strong stream of water shoots out. Used in conjunction with the brushes, it will make your glass equipment sparkle.*

- **Chlorine bleach** is widely used and very effective as cleaner and sanitizer. Two tablespoons of bleach per 3.7 liter (1 gallon) of cold water is a safe but potent mixture. Use for anything nonmetallic, as prolonged exposure to metals will cause corrosion. You can clean glass carboys by filling them with a bleach/water solution, and allowing a few days for the caustic solution to break up hardened residues. A piece of tinfoil secured with a rubber band will keep the chlorine gas from escaping. Likewise, bottles, buckets, and plastic spoons can be effectively sanitized with the solution. Bleach, however, must be used with care. Keep the following in mind when using bleach. Unless you know what you are doing, it is never a good idea to mix any chemical cleaners. Chlorine bleach produces a toxic gas when mixed with ammonia-based products. Concentrated bleach also produces unpleasant fumes. Always use bleach in a well-ventilated area. Wear expendable clothing when working with bleach, unless you find white spots on your cardigan aesthetically appealing.

- **Commercial oxidants** clean and sanitize your equipment. The recommended ratio is one tablespoon mixed with 3.7 liter (1 gallon) of water. These are great soaking agents and they won't damage metals. I often keep my empty kegs filled with one of these cleaners. Both loosen "beer stone" (hardened sediment) and keep kegs clean and ready to sanitize. Whilst most of these cleaners are environmentally friendly, you'll need to thoroughly rinse each piece of equipment after soaking. You should read the manufacturer's instructions carefully, as the directions of use for each product could vary slightly.

- **TSP** (trisodium phosphate) is a cleaner and sanitizer that must be rinsed after it is used. TSP can usually be purchased at paint-supply or hardware stores.

- **Vinegar** (acetic acid) can be used at full potency to clean any copper equipment. Use white distilled vinegar. This is great for taking the tarnish off an immersion wort chiller. Just make sure you thoroughly rinse off all of the vinegar before you place the wort chiller in your wort.

- **Grain alcohol** can be diluted with water for cleaning and sanitizing counters and tables. Fill a spray bottle with one part alcohol per five parts water, and mist and wipe the surfaces you'll be working on.

- **Iphodor** can be used to clean stainless-steel equipment, without fear of corrosion. Some homebrewers maintain that no rinsing is required after using Iphodor, though many give a quick rinse just to safeguard against off flavors. As with bleach, wear old clothing when using this sanitizer, as it can stain. One tablespoon per 19 liters (5 gallons) of water is the recommended potency.

- **Heating** equipment to temperatures above 76.7°C (170°F) will kill microorganisms. This method works well for metal objects.

- **Oven cleaner** can be used to remove carbon build-up on the bottom of your brewpot. Just be sure to neutralize the caustic agent with a weak acid. White distilled vinegar works well for this.

Bottling

▲ *Swing top bottle and standard 625 ml (22 oz) bottle.*

▶ *Bench and two-handed type bottle cappers.*

Bottles

The type of bottles you'll want to use are brown "pop-top" non-returnables. Clear and even green bottles allow a certain amount of light through. This can react with hop compounds and create a "skunky" flavor. Screw-top bottles cannot be resealed properly, and the glass is often too delicate to withstand the gaseous pressures built up during bottle conditioning.

You may also come across bottles that have swing-top plastic or ceramic resealable tops. These make bottling a breeze. Just make sure you have a supply of rubber seals to replace the old ones with when they become dry and cracked.

Bottle capper

There are a wide variety of bottle cappers available on the market. The cheapest is the hammer capper. The reason it's cheap is that it is difficult to use and can easily break bottles. The next level is the two-handed capper. These are easy to use and relatively inexpensive. This is the kind of capper that is included in most kits.

If you plan on bottling many batches of beer for many years, you'll want to invest in a bench capper. It should be adjustable to accommodate bottles of various sizes. These are so easy to use that they can actually make bottling fun.

Bottle filler and racking cane

A bottle filler is a hard plastic stem that connects to your fermenter via transfer tubing. The tip has a spring-activated point that allows beer to flow from fermenter to bottle only when pressed.

A racking cane is used during bottling and wort transfers. It is a hard, cane-shaped pipe that extends to the bottom of a carboy or bucket. Unlike soft tubing, a racking cane won't crimp (but will break if you try to bend it too hard) so that beer can flow freely. There is also a cap at the straight end with an opening about a half-inch up, to discourage the transfer of sediment.

Equipment for the home pub

Kegs

Bench capper or no bench capper, there will come a time when you will consider kegging your brew. There are several options.

Plastic pressure barrels, available in 9.5- and 22.7-liter (2·5- and 6-gallon) sizes. These use seltzer cartridges to dispense low-carbonated brew.

There is another clever system that employs citric acid and baking soda as the pumping mechanism. One case of beer fits in the plastic keg, along with the sanitary chemical pouch. As beer is drawn from the tap, the pouch expands, keeping a consistent dispensing pressure. These are used with success by many homebrewers. It is small enough to fit on a refrigerator shelf, so no extra unit is needed.

Soda keg

By far, the best system for the homebrewer is the use of a soda keg. Commonly called a Cornelius Keg (a brand name) stainless-steel soda kegs make excellent homebrewing storage and dispensing vessels. Soda kegs are durable, easy to clean, and are relatively cheap to purchase and maintain. You can find these canisters at soda-bottling distributors, restaurants, or your local homebrew supply shop.

A viable keg, shown here, should contain the following parts:

- A tight-fitting lid with a rubber gasket lining and a release handle
- In and out valve fittings
- A short gas dip tube
- A long liquid dip tube
- A pressure-release valve (some models won't have this)

THE LID

Make sure the lid is not bent or damaged. Replace the gasket if it is worn or broken.

VALVE FITTINGS

Try to find a keg that has ball-lock fittings. Inspect the O-rings on the fittings and replace them if needed. Unscrew the fittings from the keg and inspect the O-rings on the gas and liquid dip tubes. Replace these if needed. Inside the fittings you'll find little spring pressure seals called poppets. If these are worn or broken, replace them, otherwise it will be impossible to keep your keg carbonated.

SHORT GAS AND LONG LIQUID DIP TUBES

Carbon dioxide enters the keg via the gas tube and forces the liquid from the bottom of the keg up through the longer liquid tube. Remove both tubes and clean with TSP or Iphodor. If they are made of plastic, start hunting for metal replacements.

PRESSURE RELEASE VALVE

This is not found on all soda kegs, but it is very useful. Just make sure it rises a bit when pulled and returns to its original position when released.

CLEANING YOUR KEG

Clean each disassembled part, as well as the interior of the keg. Use TSP, Iphodor, or a commercial oxidant, like B-Brite. Soak all parts and rinse with warm water. Never use chlorine on metal. However, you can sanitize your rubber seals in a dilute bleach/water solution. Scrub out any residue in the keg with a carboy brush. Repeat soaking, scrubbing, and rinsing until the interior is clean and free of any lingering soft-drink and sanitizer smells. Reassemble the keg.

Connectors, hoses, and tap

There is a connector for the gas fitting and one for the liquid fitting. While they look alike, they are not interchangeable. Usually they are distinguished by color. These connect to the bulged keg fittings by a series of locking ball bearings. Once secured, connectors force the poppets down, allowing for the flow of gas and liquid. Buy your connectors new and keep them clean.

HOSES

You'll need a durable hose with an inside diameter of about 8 mm ($\frac{5}{16}$ inch) to connect your regulator to the in connector on your keg. Hardware stores sell polyethylene and vinyl gas hoses, and you can also find them at most homebrew shops. You may find it difficult to force polyethylene hose openings over the regulator out valve and the gas connector in valve. Soften the plastic by dipping the ends in hot water. Once you have both ends connected, secure each with stainless steel hose clamps.

TAP

The simplest tap is a black plastic faucet attached to a short length of tubing. These are the kind you get when you buy a keg of beer at a beverage supplier. One end of the tubing connects to the tap, the other to the liquid connector on the tank.

▼ *CO_2 tank and regulator pressure gauges.*

CO_2 tank and pressure regulator

Homebrewers often use 19-liter (5-gallon) CO_2 tanks; these fit inside small refrigerators alongside the keg and are cheap to fill. Some homebrewers, especially those who power two or more kegs at a time, prefer 76-liter (20-gallon) tanks; this cuts down on the amount of trips they have to make to the gas supplier. Check with area beverage distributors for used tanks; these should be professionally pressure-tested. Visual inspections and hydrostatic tests determine whether a tank is safe for use. If an inspector detects any flaws or weak areas on the internal aluminum canister, he or she will empty the tank and drill a hole in it. Since these tanks hold anywhere from 800 to 4,000 pounds of pressurized air per square inch, it is essential that they be safe for use.

▼ *Hook up the gas line to the keg.*

◄ *Force-carbonating beer.*

A pressure regulator controls the force of gas from the tank. Most have two gauges attached; one shows the amount of gas in the tank, and the other shows how much pressure is entering your keg. Attach your regulator to the out valve of your tank by screwing the threaded nut over the valve. There should be a plastic gasket inside the casing to assure a proper, secure seal. You can control the flow of CO_2 by turning a screw on the side of the regulator.

Keg conditioning and dispensing

Procedures for conditioning in a keg are essentially the same as those for conditioning in the bottle. The only difference is that you'll be using less priming sugar. If a recipe calls for 63 grams (⅔ cup) corn sugar for bottles, use 31.5 grams (⅓ cup) in the keg. Store your keg in a cool area for two weeks.

▲ *Hooking up the tap line.*

QUICK CARBONATION

With a little muscle and some CO_2, you can carbonate your homebrew without using priming sugar. By forcing gas into your flat beer, you can have bubbly beer in less than two days. First, cool your beer and transfer it into a sanitized keg. Hook the keg up to the tank and set the regulator to 25 psi. Pull the release valve on the keg to replace the air on the surface with CO_2. Shake the keg for about a minute. You should hear gas groaning through the regulator. This gas is being absorbed into your beer. Repeat shaking two more times, or until the sound ceases. Unhook your keg, turn off the tank, and let your homebrew settle for a day or two.

DISPENSING FROM THE KEG

Connect your keg to the gas and tap lines. Set your regulator to about 8 psi. Your first glass or two of beer may be cloudy with sediment. Pour a clear glass and check the carbonation. If your beer is flat, disconnect it from the tap and gas lines and check the lid gasket and poppets. Apply some gas and listen for leaks. Once you are assured that the keg is well sealed, force-carbonate and try again in a day or two.

Ideally, you want a steady even flow of beer, one that allows a head to form but doesn't shoot from the tap like a fire hose. At the end of the day, either disconnect the gas line from the keg and turn off the tank, or close the valve on your regulator (if yours has one) and close the tank.

Refrigerators

Now you have a CO_2 tank and regulator linked to your keg by a gas hose and connector, and a tap attached to the liquid connector from your tank. You have all the basic hardware to dispense your homebrew–now all you need is some way to cool your brew. An inexpensive and portable option is to construct a "jockey box." This is a picnic cooler that is connected inline between your keg and the tap by a length of winding copper tubing set inside. The cooler is filled with ice, which cools the beer as

▼ *Draft system.*

it flows from keg to glass. Several books provide instructions for constructing one of these handy devices. Check out *Brew Ware*, by Karl F. Lutzen and Mark Stevens for clear, detailed instructions.

A more effective, if stationary, system is to find an old refrigerator in the classified ads of your local newspaper. Any refrigerator that can maintain a temperature range of 4.4–8°C (40–48°F) is suitable for dispensing beer. Remove all plastic shelving, and be sure the inside floor can withstand the weight of a full keg and tank. Scrub any mold from the interior, and wipe with a sanitizing agent. Then, simply drill a hole in the door of the unit, feed your tap through, and seal the deal with a little silicone caulk.

Small refrigerators and freezers also make nice cooling units for your system, just make sure you can fit your keg and CO_2 tank inside. If the interior space prohibits this, you can arrange your tank outside the unit and feed the gas line through a drilled hole in the side. When drilling, always unplug your unit, and be sure you're not boring through any gas or electricity lines. Feel the surface of the plugged-in unit before you plan to drill. If it's warm to the touch you can be sure that there is more than just insulation within. Many small refrigerators contain freezer compartments that cut down on the internal space. The metal box can be removed and flipped around, giving you the headspace you need for your keg. Be sure you know what you're doing if you want to try this, however. American Brewmasters of Raleigh, NC, sell modified small refrigerators that will hold a 19-liter (5-gallon) keg and a 19-liter (5-gallon) CO_2 tank.

Small meat freezers are compact and well insulated, and thus make great dispensing coolers. Often, these have external temperature controllers that you can set to your preference. Since you don't want a "beercicle," you'll want to buy a thermostatic controller. Thermostatic controllers can be purchased through mail order, at some hardware stores, and at some homebrew supply shops. These are a good investment if you are using a freezer for dispensing beer, or if you're using a single freezer or refrigerator for the dual purpose of lagering and dispensing homebrew. Most of these devices plug into a wall outlet, and have an outlet that accepts a refrigerator plug. By attaching the controller to the side of your unit and placing the wired temperature probe within the freezer or refrigerator, you can maintain consistent temperatures.

▲ *Top-mounted tap.*

Whichever electric cooling unit you have, you can upgrade your plastic tap to a more handsome and professional-looking tap handle. You can find taps that can be mounted on either the top or side of your refrigerator. Check with your local homebrew supply shop for tap systems.

CHAPTER FIVE

Preparing to Brew

Preparing to brew

GOOD PREPARATION IS the key to successful homebrewing. This includes:

- Cleaning and sanitizing all of your equipment
- Organizing and cleaning your work area
- Having your ingredients ready for use
- Making a checklist of all the above steps

Following these steps will improve the quality of your homebrew in several ways. First, the most common source of off flavors and other problems that can plague homebrew is the presence of unwanted microorganisms. The best equipment and the finest, freshest ingredients won't compensate for unsanitary conditions. Sanitation is the foremost concern of the homebrewer. Taking extra time to ensure that all of your equipment is free of contaminants will ensure clean, great-tasting homebrew. The same goes for your work area. If the area you brew in is dirty and disorganized, you are inviting microbial visitors and ensuring a day of searching and confusion.

Are your ingredients present and accounted for? Running to the store because you don't have the extra corn sugar you thought you had will put stress on you and your brew. If you're using liquid yeast, make sure you've prepared it at least a day in advance. By having all of your ingredients ready and at arm's reach, you'll be ready when the time comes to add them to the pot or fermenter.

Finally, checklisting the above steps will provide assurance that you haven't left anything out. This chapter details each of these procedures, and illustrates how they will improve your homebrew and the fun you have brewing it.

Getting organized

Your work area

The main work area for the extract brewer is usually the kitchen. Brewers who use propane cookers may use the garage or deck as their boiling area, and then carry the wort into the kitchen to be cooled, transferred, and pitched with yeast. Many brewers store sanitized equipment in the bathroom tub. Wherever you work, you must clean and, when possible, sanitize. Indoor cleaning includes sweeping and mopping the floor, wiping down countertops with a sanitizing agent, and even misting the area with a weak bleach/water solution. Organization of your area means removing clutter and gathering all the equipment together, and having it ready for use.

Clearing away clutter means you have only the items needed for brewing around you. Dirty plates and cups should be washed and put away. Countertops should be cleared of any items that might become obstacles while you are brewing.

You should wipe down the stovetop, countertops, and any other contact surfaces with either a weak bleach/water mix or a 70:30 percent ratio of isopropyl alcohol.

Misting the room with a bleach/water solution will help cut down on the number of contaminants adrift in your work area.

▲ *Clean all surfaces with a dilute bleach/ water solution.*

The bathroom tub is a good place to store sanitized equipment. A large sanitary bucket filled with prepared equipment can be set aside in the tub until each tool is needed. Of course, you should scour your bathroom before storing equipment, mist the area with a sanitizing solution, and make sure that the toilet lid is closed.

Having an environment that is clean and organized will make your procedure easier and more fun.

Your ingredients

Only an unexpected boil-over can match the panic you'll feel if, mid-brew, you suddenly realize you forgot an ingredient, or hadn't prepared it for use. Checklist all of your ingredients. If you're using liquid yeast, prepare the packet at least a day in advance. Make sure your grains are crushed.

Finally, make a checklist of all the above steps, and be sure each is completed before you start to brew. These steps will streamline your procedure, allowing you to concentrate on brewing.

Cleaning and sanitizing your equipment

I HAVE EXPLAINED THE DIFFERENCE between cleaning and sanitation. Cleaning must always come first, as dirty equipment is impossible to sanitize. The best time to clean your equipment is right after you've brewed your latest batch. While this might seem tedious after a day of brewing, it's the best time to attack, since the sediment is still moist and easy to remove. Likewise, the best time to clean your fermenter, bucket, or glass carboy is right after you've transferred out the wort or beer.

Clean equipment must be sanitized directly prior to brewing. Sanitary tubing can collect an infectious level of airborne contaminants in a few days, as can the rest of your equipment. Summer months are especially troublesome. During muggy weather the air is thick with wild yeast and bacteria that could unleash trouble if your equipment is not thoroughly cleaned and sanitized.

There are some compounds that will both clean and sanitize your equipment (if it is relatively clean to begin with), reducing the number of janitorial steps. All of these procedures will be discussed shortly, but first a couple of important distinctions. Sanitation is the removal of most harmful microorganisms. Sterilization is the removal of all living organic material. The latter procedure is impractical and unnecessary. As long as your wort is largely free of microbes, the yeast will effectively starve its competition by draining food and oxygen resources. Then, as the level of alcohol increases during fermentation, the environment within the fermenter will become less hospitable to any remaining microorganisms. Unsanitary conditions increase the microbial competition, which utilize oxygen and food differently than do the yeast. Other, less pleasant compounds are formed by bacteria and wild yeast, none of which you want in your beer. However, don't be worried about accidentally creating a poisonous brew. There are no known pathogens that can exist in beer. Concentrate instead on brewing a batch that won't leave a bad taste in your mouth.

There are two phases of the homebrewing process: the hot side and the cold side. The hot side includes equipment used up to the boil and down to where the wort cools to 60°C (140°F). Here, sanitation is not a major concern. The heat of an extended boil will eliminate all microorganisms. Just make sure your equipment is free of any soap or chemical residues that may impart undesirable characteristics to your brew. During the cold side, sanitation is crucial. Cool wort is an ideal breeding ground for bacteria and wild yeast. Everything that comes into contact with wort or beer at temperatures lower than 60°C (140°F) must be sanitized.

Equipment used during the hot side includes the brewpot and lid, stirring spoon, strainer, immersion thermometer, and grain and hops bags. Each of these should be clean and free of any residue before you brew. Here's how to do it.

Hot-side equipment
BREWPOT AND LID

Brewpots can be cleaned with a mild, scent-free hand-dishwashing detergent and a soft sponge. Stubborn deposits can be removed by filling the brewpot with hot water for an hour and then using a plastic scrubbing pad to dislodge the residue. If gunk in your brewpot is especially tenacious, try soaking it in *one* of the following mixtures. A–one tablespoon of TSP per 3.7 liters (1 gallon) of hot water is a very effective cleaner. Limit the exposure of this solution to under an hour. B–most commercial oxidants contain peroxides that will break up any stubborn organic deposits. These are nontoxic and safe to use on metal. However, rinse off all traces of the slippery residue before you use your brewpot. The lid can usually be easily cleaned using a little unscented hand-dishwashing detergent and a sponge. Since both pot and lid will be subjected to high heat, you don't have to worry about sanitation. Just make sure that each is thoroughly rinsed of any detergent residue. Both beer and detergent can foam up, yet the two mixed will create a brew with no foamy head.

After several homebrew sessions, you may notice a slight patina of tarnish developing on the inside of your brewpot. This is not really a concern. It won't negatively affect your beer.

STIRRING SPOON

Wood is not generally recommended for stirring cool wort, because its porous nature will nurture bacteria. Wood can be used for the hot side, though. So can food-grade plastic and stainless steel. Clean your spoons after each homebrew session, before any gunk can harden on them. A quick washing in warm water before you begin your next batch is sufficient preparation. Try to use brewing spoons only for brewing and keep them clean and free of nicks and scratches.

STRAINER

These can be cleaned in the same fashion as the brewpot. If you have reservations about sparging hot liquid through your grains via the strainer, you can sanitize the strainer. If it is made entirely of metal, simply boil it for 15 minutes. You can wipe plastic-sided strainers with a dilute solution of bleach water (1 tbsp per 19 liters/ 5 gal.). However, all liquid passed through the strainer will eventually be boiled, killing any microorganisms from either the grain or the strainer. Strainers used for pouring cool wort into the fermenter must be sanitized.

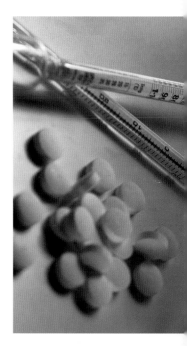

▲ *It is vital that any thermometer used during the brewing process is sanitized.*

THERMOMETER

Make sure there is no stuck-on debris, the boil will take care of the rest. If you are using a second thermometer for cold-side temperature readings, it must be sanitized.

GRAIN AND HOPS BAGS

Hops bags are meant to be disposable. Simply fill them with hops, drop them in the wort, and when the time comes, extract them and throw the bags away. Nylon grain bags can be reused, but should be cleaned by boiling after each use. Hops bags used for dry hopping must be sanitized. This is easily accomplished by boiling the empty bag for 10–15 minutes.

Cold-side equipment

Once your wort drops below 60°C (140°F), all conditions and equipment must be sanitary. Some labs actually use malt-extract concentrates to develop strains of micro-organisms. The warm, nutritious solution is an ideal environment for cultivation. However, you don't have to don a lab coat to avoid microbial intrusion. Just make a habit of keeping your equipment and environment clean and sanitary.

The list of equipment used during the cold side is longer than the one detailing the previous phase. It includes such procedures as wort cooling, transfer into primary and secondary fermenters, yeast pitching, and bottling or kegging. All equipment used for these steps must be sanitary. Perfectly good wort or beer can be spoiled if it comes into contact with a contamination source. So to repeat ad nauseam: sanitize, sanitize, sanitize!

Here's how to clean and sanitize equipment used during the cold side.

Carefully inspect all of your equipment. Is your plastic fermenter stained? Are there traces of sediment lining the inside of your transfer tubing? Does the copper tubing of your immersion wort chiller look dirty and rusty? Pay close attention to detail. Stains, tarnish, and organic residues harbor bacteria that cannot be reached by sanitizing agents. Rid your soiled equipment of these deposits so that they can be properly sanitized. Cleaning usually includes a sponge or pad, a little detergent, and a lot of wiping and scrubbing. However, different materials require different methods. You won't want to use a carboy brush on the soft interior of your bucket, and you can't use a sponge to reach the inside areas of bottles or carboys. The chlorine solution you used for sanitizing your carboy is not the solution for a sparkling soda keg. Here are some popular methods for cleaning and sanitizing cold-side equipment.

▲ *The inside and outside of plastic tubing should be completely clean.*

PLASTICS

This includes fermentation buckets, transfer and blow-off tubing, racking cane and bottle filler, spigots, airlocks and rubber stoppers, and plastic stirring spoons. First, make sure none of these items are scratched or nicked. If they are, throw them away. Plastic items are usually cheap, but unsanitizable materials can be quite costly. You're investing money, time, and love into your craft, so don't allow hidden bacteria to spoil your brew. Clean your plastic fermenter by wiping it with a sponge soaked in the bleach/water solution. If those stains remain, fill the bucket with either the bleach solution or with a commercial oxidant, and allow the chemicals to do their thing. Any of these can be left in the fermenter for an extended period of time, though bleach usually gets the job done in less than an hour. Next, empty the bucket and wipe out the residue. If you're using one of the commercial oxidants, rinse with hot, then warm, then cold water.

Sanitizing a clean bucket is easily accomplished with a half-hour soaking with the bleach/water solution. Before you start to brew, simply pour out the liquid, put the uncovered bucket in a clean indoor spot, and allow it to air-dry. Most of the chlorine will drift from the dry bucket in its normal gas state. If you are concerned about extra chlorine affecting the fermentation process or the taste of your final beer, you can quickly rinse the bucket using pre-boiled water. The lid can be cleaned and sanitized along with the bucket. Wipe it with the sponge, paying special attention to the underside, the airlock hole, and the rubber seal around the inside rim.

If you have a spigot attached to your bucket, you may want to remove it for cleaning and sanitizing. The threads that screw onto the inner gasket can become filled with malt and hop residue. Soak all parts in a bleach solution to loosen the sediment. Next, dip a cotton swab into the solution and clean out the grooved surfaces. While you're giving this area particular attention stick a pre-dipped cotton swab up the nozzle of the spigot to clean its interior. Finally, soak the attachments in another bleach solution for a half-hour, rinse with pre-boiled water if desired, and replace it on the bucket.

A vigorous fermentation can belch residue into your airlock and stain your rubber stopper. Clean and sanitize these with methods similar to those above.

Plastic tubing can be quite troublesome to maintain, making the most intrepid souls a bit neurotic. Both the inside and outside of transfer and blow-off tubing are exposed to the brew at some point, so each must be clean and free of pests. The outside can be readily wiped, but the inside is more difficult to access. Yet even small traces of grime can house communities of bacteria, so the inside has to be as clean as the outside. How can this be done?

Soak the tubing in a diluted oxidant for an hour or so to loosen any caked-on material. Next, dip a piece of paper towel in the same solution and twist it into a shape that will just fit into one end of the tubing. Using water from either your sink or garden hose (the latter is recommended) force the paper towel through the tubing until it spits out at the other end. Now, repeat this process starting at the opposite end of the tubing. This should rid your hose of debris. Thoroughly rinse the inside and outside of the tubing until all traces of cleaner are gone. If your tubing doesn't squeak when you rub it, it's not completely rinsed. Sanitize the tubing in a bleach solution and hang to dry. Ceiling hooks work great for this, as they keep the tubing from coming into contact with other surfaces.

▼ *Use a carboy brush to eliminate any residue.*

Your racking cane and bottle filler should be soaked in a bleach/water solution.

GLASS

Glass equipment includes carboys, bottles, thermometers, and hydrometers. You don't need to worry about the last item, because any wort or beer extracted for a hydrometer reading will not be introduced back into the source. Still, you should regularly clean your hydrometer with warm water to keep the balanced scale accurate.

If you're using a separate glass thermometer for post-boil (cold-side) readings it must be clean and sanitary. Clean it as you did for the thermometer used for the boil. Sanitize in a container of bleach solution for a half-hour and wipe with a new sponge that has been dipped in the same solution. Keep it in a safe environment until you're ready to take any temperature readings. My advice is to keep your hot-side thermometer in the brewpot during all phases of the boil. The same thermometer can be kept in the pot after the boil to monitor the temperature of the cooling wort. Use a second one to measure the temperature of water used for dry yeast rehydration and the temperature of the wort sample used for hydrometer measurement.

You can clean your carboy by filling it with either a commercial oxidant or a bleach/water solution, then scrubbing out all organic residues with a carboy brush. Bottle washers are also helpful for "power-washing" the interior surfaces. Once the glass sparkles, sanitize it with a bleach solution and let it air-dry. If you want to rinse the carboy, use pre-boiled cooled water. Boiling-hot water can crack a glass carboy.

You can store a sanitized carboy indefinitely by placing a piece of tinfoil over the mouth and securing it with a rubber band.

Bottles can pose a dilemma. Brown bottles are best for storing homebrew, and yet the protection from a beer-spoiling light afforded by the color also makes it difficult to see deposits that must be removed prior to sanitation. The easiest way to circumvent this problem is to purchase clean, unlabeled bottles at a homebrew supply shop and keep them clean by rinsing each one thoroughly after you decant its contents into a glass.

If you obtain bottles from a bar or restaurant, chances are they'll require a lot of cleaning. You should use a bottle washer and a bottle brush to clean the insides. Constant rinsing, scrubbing, and inspection against a strong light will ensure your bottles are free of debris.

▲ *Bottles need to be cleaned thoroughly.*

Wherever you get your bottles, you'll need to sanitize them before use. Again, a bleach/water solution is great for snuffing out microscopic gremlins. You can employ a new plastic trashcan as a holding tank for a couple of dozen bottles. Fill the trashcan three-quarters full of bleach/water solution, and dump your cleaned bottles in. Secure the lid and wait a day or two. If you are using labeled bottles, you should remove the paper and glue before you put them in the trashcan. In his book, *Dave Miller's Homebrewing Guide*, Miller suggests using an ice scraper and some ammonia to remove labels. This is an effective procedure, but note the following carefully. Make sure all traces of ammonia are rinsed off the bottles before immersing them in chlorine. *Chlorine and ammonia produce a toxic gas when mixed!* Rinse, rinse, and then rinse the bottles some more. Also, ammonia alone can be unpleasant to work with. Try to remove your labels outside where the fumes will readily dissipate.

On the day you bottle, scoop out all the bottles from the trashcan and allow them to air-dry. Once dry, they are ready to fill.

METAL

Metal equipment used during the cold side includes wort chillers, funnels, spoons, and kegs. Bleach and water can't be used to clean these items as chlorine corrodes metal, causing pitting and pinholes, perfect places for bacteria to breed.

Counterflow wort chillers must be cleaned immediately after use by pumping a large volume of boiling water through the copper lines. Immersion wort chillers can be cleaned using white distilled vinegar and a plastic scrubbing pad. This will keep your copper clean and in mint condition. Just be sure to rinse the coils with water to remove any traces of acetic acid. You can sanitize your clean immersion wort chiller by placing it in the brewpot during the last 20 minutes of the boil.

Metal funnels can be cleaned using TSP or a commercial oxidant. After a brief soaking in one of these solutions, scrub the funnel with a plastic scrubbing pad. Sanitize by either boiling the funnel in water for 20 minutes, or soaking it in an Iphodor solution. Be careful—iodine stains clothing!

The easiest way to clean a stainless-steel spoon is to scrub it under warm water. You can sanitize it by boiling the metal for 20 minutes. Just be sure not to boil any nonmetallic parts, like a plastic handle.

Soda kegs can be cleansed using a diluted commercial oxidant. Once the keg is empty, rinse out any residue and fill it with the above-mentioned solution. Store the keg with the lid secured until it's time to keg your next batch.

CHAPTER SIX

Intermediate Brewing

Intermediate brewing techniques

THIS CHAPTER WILL introduce advanced concepts and techniques aimed at helping you produce better beer. Some terms that have been glossed over earlier will be explored in greater detail, and you will be introduced to some new procedures. This section is intended for the brewer who has reached a level of ease and comfort with novice procedures, and is ready to step up his or her knowledge and brewing system. Here you will learn how to make partial-mash homebrew, how to predict actual bitterness, how to adjust the mineral content of your brew liquor, and more. Intermediate brewing is more demanding than extract brewing, but it's not brain surgery either. You don't need to master chemistry or memorize Latin to make superior brew. You just need a thirst that commonly increases among homebrewers to learn, experiment, and have fun. The only mistake a homebrewer can make is to decide that he or she can't progress toward more complex procedures. Barring bacterial infection, all botched brew can be drunk. Furthermore, the more you brew, the better your product will become. So don't fear. Enjoy the process, learn from your mistakes, and enjoy the beer you create.

Meditating on malt

NOW WE'LL TURN our attention back to grains–using and understanding them–and we'll also look at predicting specific gravity and color.

Much to the bewilderment of contented extract brewers, some roguish, restless adventurers insist on using grains as the whole of their grist. They'll spend weeks grappling with junkyard scrap, hammering and tinkering in the garage, constructing the internal, eternal dream of the perfect all-grain system. What's more, they will happily sacrifice eight to ten hours mashing and sparging, hovering over their devices like medieval alchemists trying to turn base metal into gold. Yet so often they succeed. And we extract brewers who puzzle over such labor admit with leaden hearts that these alchemists have created a superior elixir.

Partial-mash brewing

What advantage do brewers who use grain have over those who use only extract? Well, for one they have greater control. Even with extracts of the highest quality, we are partly confined by the contents of the package. Extract brewing *is* real brewing, but the brewer lacks the range available to those who add grains. Partial-mash brewing is the link between the novice and the advanced brewer. By adding fermentable grains and adjuncts to your extract, you will gain the freshness and range of style and nuance enjoyed by all-grain brewers.

There are many ways you can add grain to your extract to improve the quality of your beer. Earlier, I showed you how to add specialty grains to enhance the character of your extract homebrew. Specialty grains don't require mashing. You are simply deriving color, flavor, and body from the small additions. Partial-mash brewing requires that you mash the grains prior to adding them to the brewpot. By mashing, you are converting modified starches into dextrins and sugars, while taking care not to extract tannins from the grain husk. Besides the pride you will gain in knowing that you successfully converted starch to sugar, you will notice your homebrew take on a fresher flavor. Once you see how easy mashing can be, you may even decide to venture into the ultimate practice of professionals and advanced homebrewers: all-grain brewing.

All-grain brewers use three popular mashing procedures: single infusion, step mashing, and decoction mashing. Each method attempts to utilize two major enzymes (among others) within the malt: alpha amylase and beta amylase. Both enzymes break down long chains of carbohydrates into fermentable compounds. However, each works differently and both are activated at dissimilar temperatures. Alpha amylase breaks down compounds somewhat randomly. It may disconnect the molecules in the center of the chain or near the ends, creating smaller chunks of glucose chains. Alpha amylase is most active at a temperature range of 65.6–70°C (150–58°F). Beta amylase methodically shears off glucose molecules at the ends of the long carbohydrate chains. This enzyme works at lower temperatures, with the high end being around 60°C (140°F). Both enzymes are needed to fully convert starches into sugars. By far the most simple and popular mashing method is the single-infusion mash. This simply means that the malt is added at a temperature that makes use of both enzymes. While step mashing and decoction mashing traditionally promote a more thorough starch conversion, the well-modified malts that are available today work fine with the single-infusion method.

There are two popular techniques for single-infusion partial-mash brewing. Both require some extra equipment, and a little added time. For each method, I recommend the use of a propane gas burner and an accurate, reliable thermometer. A high-BTU burner offers much more control than any range-heating element. Metal probe thermometers work well, as they respond to temperature changes more quickly than glass mercury thermometers.

PREPARING YOUR GRAINS

Before you mash you must properly crush the grains. Proper crushing means you extrude and crumble the interior of the grain, while leaving the husks intact and whole. The ideal would be that you turn the endosperm into tiny granules and leave the husk as if it were an empty sack. This would allow the starches maximum exposure to the brew liquor, resulting in a complete conversion, while keeping the tannin-rich husk out of the mash and using it as an effective filter bed during lautering and sparging. Commercial breweries use large, expensive roller mills to get the job done. Since you are using only a small amount of grain, you have a few less expensive options.

Many homebrew supply shops have grain crushers on the premises. If you decide to use one of these mills, make sure there is no residual material in the machine. Run it empty for half a minute while you shake the outlet tube. This should clear the mill of any dust and debris. By the way, be courteous and collect this material in a bag. Empty the bag, place it under the outlet tube, and pour in your grains. Once all of the grain is transferred into the bag, turn off the mill and clear it for the next customer.

There are several electric and manual roller mills on the market which range in price. For a small amount of money you can pick up a Corona Mill that can be adjusted to give your grains the crush they need. The mill crushes by forcing grain between two grooved plates, one of which is rotated by hand. You'll need to adjust the gap between the plates to achieve a proper crush. If you're grinding out powder, the plates are too close together. Conversely, if grains are tumbling through unscathed, you'll need to tighten the gap. The plates are quickly and easily adjustable, so fiddle around with them until your grain comes out right.

Method One: steeping and sparging

This procedure is almost identical to the addition of specialty grains, and in fact, both additions can be mixed and employed simultaneously. In addition to the extra equipment recommended above, all you'll need is a large strainer, a grain-steeping bag (optional), a 7.5-liter (2-gallon) saucepan, and about 1.8-liters (½-gallon) of extra water that has been pre-heated to 76.7°C (170°F). Here is a step-by-step explanation.

1 Heat 1.8–2.8 liters (½–¾ gallons) of water in the saucepan to about 70°C (158°F). Add your grains (in the steeping bag or loose) and maintain a temperature of 66.7–70°C (152–58°F). Let this mixture stand for about 45 minutes.
2 Place a larger strainer over your brewpot and pour the grains and liquid into the strainer, allowing the liquid to filter into the pot.
3 Now slowly pour the 1.8 liters (½ gallon) of preheated water over grains.
4 Remove any floating husks from the brewpot, add water, and brew as usual.

▲ You can add specialty malt grains directly to your brewpot at the same time as you begin the partial-mash brew process.

That's really all there is to mashing. By heating the water to 70°C (158°F), you are allowing both major enzymes to do their thing. Maintaining the above temperature range for 45 minutes facilitates starch-to-sugar conversion. Sparging the grains with 76.7°C (170°F) water rinses excess sugars from the grain, while keeping tannins from the grain husk from dissolving into the pot. Lynne O'Conner, proprietor of St Patrick's brewing supply in Texas, teaches apprehensive extract brewers this simple method, to help them overcome their fear of mashing.

▶ In a professional brewery the motorized rakes gently agitate the grain within the mash/lauter tun.

Method Two: using a lauter tun

The second method is a bit more complex. It requires the use of a 19-liter (5-gallon) lauter bucket, a 19-liter (5-gallon) fermenting bucket with a spigot, some transfer tubing, and a tincture of iodine. A lauter bucket is simply a food-grade plastic bucket with several dozen small holes drilled into the bottom. This fits into the fermenting bucket with the spigot. The transfer tubing allows a smooth transfer of liquid from the bucket into the brewpot. The iodine is used to test for starch conversion. When iodine comes into contact with starch, it turns from yellow to blue or purple-black, depending on the starch concentration. If you want to see this in action, pour a small amount of iodine onto a saucer. Dip a bit of bread in and you'll notice a drastic color change. The starches in the bread react with the iodine causing the change in color. Don't eat this bread. Iodine is toxic.

◄ *Lauter bucket and sieve*

▶ *Transfer tubing.*

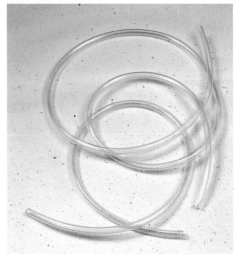

1

Heat 2.8–3.7 liters
(¾–1 gallon) of water
to 71.1˚C (160°F).

2

Add your grains and
steep for about 45
minutes.

4

Stir the liquid as it
steeps.

3

Maintain a
temperature range of
66.7–70˚C
(152–158°F).

5

Using a turkey baster
or a ladling spoon,
extract a small sample
of wort from the mash,
taking care not to pick
up any floating grain
husks.

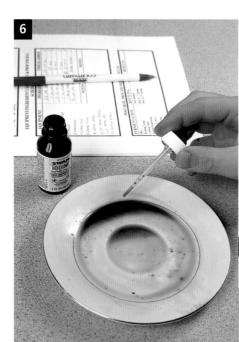

Pour this into a plate and add a few drops of iodine. If the solution turns blue or purple, there are still starches in the pot and mashing should continue.

Repeat this test periodically until there is no change in the sample. *Note:* do not *introduce the test wort back into the mashing pot. Pour it down the sink and rinse the plate.*

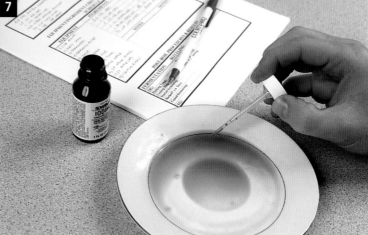

When mashing is complete, pour into the lauter bucket, which should be fitted into a fermenting bucket. Make sure the spigot is closed.

Now, slowly draw off about 236 ml (1 cup) of liquid into a clear measuring cup. You'll probably notice that the sample is cloudy.

10

Gently pour the sample back into the lauter bucket and repeat the process until the wort looks relatively clear.

11

Now connect the transfer tubing to the spigot and direct the other end into your brewpot.

12

Slowly siphon the liquid into the pot, while matching the flow with the preheated water. Don't dump the water over the grains; sprinkle evenly. Once all the liquid is collected into the brewpot, add water and brew as usual.

Mashing at the above temperature range allows both enzymes to work. Be sure to keep your temperature within this range. Excessive heat will draw tannins from the grain husks, and, more disconcertingly, you will denature ("kill") the enzymes, making starch-to-sugar conversion impossible. By pouring the grain mixture into the lauter bucket, and slowly drawing off samples, you are creating a natural filter bed using the grain husks. As you continue to lauter, the sponge-like bed is collecting particles and large compounds that would otherwise cause haze and other problems in your beer. Gentle sparging rinses the excess sugars from the grain, maximizing your yield.

This method is recommended for larger grain additions and is more similar to the procedure all-grain brewers use than the first method. While both methods are suitable for relatively small grain additions, the latter will result in a more complete extraction of sugars and dextrins, and will produce a clearer wort. Specialty grains can be added with mashing grains in either method.

Predicting gravity and color

Using the malt profiles table in the back of this book, you can gain a rough estimate of the original gravity and color your malt additions will give to your homebrew. As you read this section and the sections on hop bitterness predictions and yeast, keep in mind that your primary goal is to make delicious homebrew. Don't get so bogged down in predictions and calculations that you lose focus of this objective. Your mission is to have fun and enjoy your homebrew. With that in mind, let's explore the specifics of gravity and the spectrum of colorful possibility awaiting you and your brew.

FEELING GRAVITY'S PULL

Predicting original gravity is simple and inevitably somewhat inaccurate. To calculate original gravity, you are merely multiplying the gravities proffered by the various malts, sugars, and adjuncts by the amount of each addition that will enter your pot, adding the totals, and dividing the sum by the volume of finished beer (five gallons, in our case). For example, say you are adding 6.6 pounds of amber malt extract syrup and a pound of crystal malt. Looking up the respective gravities in the Malt Profiles Table you find that one pound of the syrup yields about 1·040 per gallon of water and the crystal malt affords 1·030 per gallon. Dropping the decimals, you have 40 and 30. Your equation would look like this:

$$40 \times 6 \cdot 6 = 264$$
$$30 \times 1 = \underline{30}$$
$$294/5 = 58.8 \text{ or an OG of } 1 \cdot 059$$

This is dicey business. First, extract syrups and powders tend to offer gravity ranges rather than one specific, fixed number. Second, crushing and mashing methods will dictate how much of the theoretical maximum of gravity you'll get from any grain. No honest professional brewers or homebrewers will claim to get one hundred percent of the potential gravity. This is because no brewing system is perfect.

To gauge the efficiency of your system, look up one of the recipes in this or another book. Calculate the original gravity using the formula above and check it against the original gravity offered with the recipe. Divide the recipe original gravity by the theoretical maximum and you'll get an efficiency percentage, usually around 85 percent. Now make that beer. Check your OG and divide that by the theoretical max. Now you'll have some idea about the comparative efficiency of your system.

Keep in mind that different brands of extract may yield different original gravities. If a recipe calls for John Bull extract, you may get a higher or lower yield by using another brand. One final caveat: when you brew with a concentrated wort and dilute it with water, you may not get an accurate OG. Water and wort do not instantly blend into a homogeneous solution. The larger the amount of wort you can actually boil, the more accurate your reading will be.

APPROXIMATING COLOR

Predicting color is even more perplexing than predicting gravity. In the US, Standard Reference Method (SRM) is used to analyze beer color. The SRM scale is based on an older system called the Lovibond scale, which measured malt color. Often, you'll see Lovibond ratings on malt and grain. For practical purposes, the two scales are the same. Accurate SRM measurement requires the use of a spectrophotometer. If you do not have a spectrophotometer, you may be able to procure one by placing a second mortgage on your house. Barring this potentially relationship-breaking decision, you'll have to rely on other means for predicting and analyzing color.

Color in liquid is not the same as color on a solid. To test this, pour most of a homebrew into your favorite glass. Now pour the remainder into your hydrometer vial. Hold the two samples up to a light source. Your glass of brew will appear darker. Why? The larger volume of beer allows less light to pass through, effecting a deeper color. Next, pour the two samples into the sink. Just kidding. Drink them.

SRM is simply a scale that helps define the lightness or darkness of a beer. It is in no way a substitute for the human eye. SRM does not reveal subtleties of hue, and cannot differentiate between a yellow or light gold beer. Therefore, in addition to assigning a beer to an SRM range, brewers and beer judges often use words to convey variances that are too fine to be captured by the scale. For example, a witbier and a Pilsner have SRM ratings between 2 and 4·5. Yet, witbier is a pale, almost flat-looking yellow, while a Pilsner's yellow is effulgent. This is due to the ingredients and process involved in making the two beers. The SRM scale certainly works for beer styles with dramatically different colors. An opaque stout has an SRM rating of over 40, while a pale to golden weizen ranges between 3 and 10.

A good weekend experiment is to gather together some friends and purchase the following beer styles: wit (2–4 SRM) Pils (3–4·5 SRM), weizen (3–10 SRM), India pale ale (7–14 SRM), brown ale (14–35 SRM), porter (30–45 SRM), and dry stout (35–70 SRM). Pour the same amount of each into identical glasses. Now line them up with a light source behind them, and study the differences in color. Notice the shades of burgundy catching the edges of the porter, as the staunch stout collects all light like a silky black hole. Note the copper color of the IPA next to the deeper color of the brown ale. The spectrum of colors will offer you some perspective on the use and limitations of the color scale.

One way to approximate color is by using Homebrew Color Units (HCUs). Simply multiply the SRM or Lovibond rating assigned to each ingredient called for in the recipe by how much of that malt or adjunct you use. Add the totals and divide by the volume of beer (19 liters/5 gallons). This will give you a *rough* estimate of final beer color. Of course, extracts rarely give specific color ratings, and factors such as length of boil, concentration of wort, cooling rate, fermentation conditions, and finings all obscure the calculations. Still, like the formula used to approximate OG, HCUs will give you some idea of how your beer will end up looking.

The best way to learn color approximation is through experience. Brew styles of different color, keeping good records on the worksheets. Notice how different percentages of various malts blend to create color. Become familiar with the colors of specialty malts. Use calculations to point you in the right direction, but rely on the instinct that comes with experience to fine-tune your palette.

Entering the cone

HERE'S WHERE WE'LL take a closer look at the role of hops in homebrewing. Hops are used to balance the sweet malt and to add flavor and aroma to your final beer. Alpha acids are responsible for the bitterness, while essential oils furnish flavor and bouquet. Let's examine both of these valuable hop components, and see how you can maximize and specify the characteristics proffered by each.

Alpha acids

Hops contain both hard resins and soft resins. Hard resins are not soluble, even with the addition of heat, and therefore contribute nothing to the bitterness of beer. Soft resins are divided into several groups, including alpha and beta acids. As we saw earlier, under normal conditions beta acids are not soluble and don't contribute much to beer. However, prolonged exposure to air oxidizes hop resins, minimizing the effects of alpha acids and amplifying the effects of beta acids. Beta acids lend a harsher, less pleasing bitterness to beer, so proper storage is important to decrease their effects.

Alpha acids are composed of three major components: humulone, cohumulone, and adhumulone.

Researchers are still studying the specific role each of these three compounds plays in supplying bitterness. Cohumulone has been found to be the most soluble of the three, and is said to impart a harsher bitterness than humulone and adhumulone. While the concentrations of these compounds vary from harvest to harvest, higher-alpha hops tend to contain more cohumulone. For this reason, some brewers are favoring larger additions of lower-alpha hops to achieve proper bittering levels to give less harsh aftertaste.

Alpha-acid utilization

Alpha Acid Units give you some idea how much bitterness is entering your wort. However, it is important to understand that only a small percentage of alpha acid remains in the wort. Only alpha acids that have gone through the chemical rearrangement known as isomerization end up in your fermenter. Even isomerized alpha acids can be lost through fermentation, filtration, and the addition of fining agents. An optimistic calculation of hop utilization is around 30 percent. The rest are lost in the boil and the processes that follow. What are some of the variables that affect hop utilization?

Length of boil • Wort gravity • Hopping rate • Freshness of the hops • Vigorous fermentation • Hot break and cold break • Yeast sedimentation • Filtration • Water hardness.

Predicting bitterness: IBUs

International Bittering Units (IBUs) measure the amount of iso-alpha acids in beer. One IBU, or simply BU, equals one milligram per liter of iso-alpha acid in solution. This figure can be analyzed in laboratories; however, you can gain a rough estimate by using a predictive formula. If AAUs tell you how much bitterness is going into your brewpot, IBU formulas predict how much will actually be utilized. Several knowledgeable brewers have created formulas and tables designed to predict IBUs. Byron Burch, Randy Mosher, Jackie Rager, and Mark Garetz have all published calculation tables. I have chosen to use a relatively new formula devised by Glenn Tinseth. I like his method because it is not too complex, yet I have found it useful in my own brewing experience. The two main empirical factors he takes into account are wort gravity and boil time (the time hops spend in the boil). Using his utilization table (see page 137) and a simple formula, you can calculate how many IBUs you will attain by adding a given amount of hops with various alpha-acid percentages. Using this method, along with the Beer Style Guidelines, you can formulate your own methods for attaining proper bitterness levels as required by specific styles.

Here is how Tinseth's formula works:

Say you are brewing a batch of your favorite homebrew that has an original gravity of 1·060. You are bittering with two ounces of Northern Brewer (NB) hops with an alpha acid content of 8 percent. You plan on adding one ounce for 60 minutes and the other for 30 minutes. How many IBUs will this yield? Here is the basic formula:

IBUs = decimal alpha acid utilization x mg/l of added alpha acids

Using Tinseth's chart, we see that the alpha-acid utilization for the additions are 0·211 for the NB hops boiled for 60 minutes and 0·162 for those boiled for 30 minutes. To calculate mg/liter of added alpha acids, use the following formula:

$$\textbf{mg/l of added alpha acids} = \frac{\textbf{decimal AA rating x oz hops x 7490}}{\textbf{volume of finished beer in gallons}}$$

SO

$$\textbf{mg/l of added alpha acids} = \frac{\textbf{0·08(8\% AA) x 2(oz) x 7490}}{\textbf{5 gallons}}$$

Equals: 239·68

Divide this number by half, as you are adding in stages: 119·84

Now plug this number into the IBU formula:

For the 60-minute addition: **IBUs = 0·211 x 119·84**, or about 26 IBUs
For the 30-minute addition: **IBUs = 0·162 x 119·84,** or about 19 IBUs
Adding these two numbers together, you come up with 45 IBUs

If you want to lower the number of IBUs you can either add less hops or use a variety with a lower alpha-acid percentage. In the first case the ounces will be your variable, and in the second case, alpha-acid percentage is the unknown. Since you already have the utilization numbers, simply plug these variables into the equation.

If you want to lower your IBUs by cutting your additions by, say one-quarter, you'll be adding 1·5 oz NB hops with an AA% of 8. To find mg/l of added alpha acids, simply substitute 1·5 oz for 2 oz. Some quick calculations will give you 179·76. Divide this in half and plug these numbers into 60- and 30- minute additions: about 19 IBUs for the 60-minute addition and about 15 IBUs for those added at the 30-minute mark for a total of 34 IBUs. If you are using a lower-alpha-acid hop, simply apply the new percentage into the equation, keeping the amount of added hops the same (2 oz).

The essence of oils

No two snowflakes are alike, no two jazz saxophonists play a tune the same, and no two types of hops impart the same flavor and aroma to your cool beverage. There are dozens of hop varieties available to the homebrewer, and each contains a different concentration of the volatile oils that affect your brew. Cascade and Saaz are both vine-growing varieties of *Humulus lupulus*, but no one can argue that they taste the same in the glass. Diverse forms of the same hop, and when and how they are introduced, will impart different characteristics. Some brewers add flavoring hops within the last few minutes of the boil. Others filter their hot wort through whole-hop beds before cooling, to pick up aromas and flavors. A different bouquet is achieved by introducing pellet, plug, or whole hops into your secondary fermenter. What makes for such a wide range of scent and taste?

All plants contain oils. Some are fixed, others volatile. Volatile oils evaporate into the air and dissolve into solution. These are the oils that provide pungence and piquancy. Hop researchers have identified 22 essential oil components that influence the flavor and aroma of beer. These are subdivided into three groups: Humulene and Caryophyllene Oxidation products, Floral-Estery Compounds, and Citrus-Piny Compounds. These appear, in varying proportions, in the prized aroma hops that homebrewers use to crown their beer.

Fleecing the fleeting oils

Since these oils are volatile, they tend to dissipate quickly. Poorly stored hops, or hops that have endured a prolonged boil, will contribute little flavor and aroma to the finished product. Follow the storage recommendations for hops to preserve the delicate oils. Constrain any finishing hop additions to the final 20 minutes of the total boil. The longer you leave them in, the less good they'll do. Also, cover the pot after you add these hops. This may reintroduce any vaporized aromas back into the brewpot. Finally, proper brewing procedure will discourage the introduction of oxygen at the wrong time. Oxidation affects many compounds in your wort and beer, and hop oils are no exception. For a complete study on hop oils, visit Glenn Tinseth's Hop Page on the World Wide Web at www.Realbeer.com.

Attenuation, please: another look at yeast

Even the most fanatical homebrewer must eventually step away from the fermenter and let the yeast go to work. Fermentation, aging, and conditioning normally work best without human intervention, save prayers, incantations, and good luck rituals. Homebrewers merely set fermentation into motion. After this, we are spectators. However, not all fermentation goes as planned. Sometimes the yeast seem to take forever to begin working. Other times, fermentation rolls on ceaselessly in a never-ending plop of bubbles through the airlock. You may see a batch that starts fermenting strong and swift, then suddenly stops. Such symptoms may be traced to bacterial infection, underpitching, or improper fermentation temperatures. By far, pitching too little yeast is the cause of most fermentation problems. Long lag times, high final gravity, and even the occasional bacterial coup may result from underpitching. If these sound familiar, pitch more yeast the next time around.

Always pitch enough yeast

At the height of fermentation, there are roughly 50 million yeast cells per milliliter of wort. After this, the yeast cells start to drop from suspension into a bed of sediment and become dormant.

The desired pitching rate for the purposes of homebrewing is in the range of 5 to 10 million cells per milliliter of wort for ales and even more for lagers. Underpitching puts a strain on yeast that might result in long lag times (the quiet period between pitching and apparent fermentation), protracted fermentation times, and stuck fermentation.

If you want to know how thoroughly your yeast strain is attenuating the fermentables in the primary you can use the following formula:

AAP (Apparent Attenuation Percentage) = [(original gravity – final gravity)/ original gravity] x 100

For example, if the original gravity of your wort is 1·060 and the final gravity of the beer is 1·020, the equation would look like this (drop the decimals on the gravity readings):

$$\text{AAP} = \frac{(60-20)}{40} = 0{\cdot}666 \times 100 = 67\% \text{ apparent attenuation}$$

If your readings fall below this range, your yeast is not fully attenuating. This may well be the result of pitching too little yeast. Keep in mind that lager yeast will ferment a broader range of wort sugars and typically has a higher attenuation percentage. You can easily up the amount of yeast that goes into the fermenter by making a yeast starter. As you'll see, this is not hard to do.

Preparing a yeast starter: avoid culture shock

Yeast starters work by gradually introducing yeast to larger and larger volumes of wort. Once the liquid pack is prepared, the yeast cells thrive within a small amount of sterile wort. However, the yeast colony is still young and vulnerable. A yeast starter is a slightly larger volume of sanitary wort that allows the yeast to further strengthen and multiply before taking the 19-liter (5-gallon) plunge. Considering it takes a day or two for a liquid packet to "strengthen" and a day extra for the starter to become viable, you should plan these procedures two to three days before you brew.

To make a yeast starter you'll need the following items:

- A 3.7-liter (1-gallon) bottle that will accept a rubber stopper and airlock (empty "growlers," containers brewpubs use to sell draft beer, work well)
- A drilled rubber stopper and airlock
- 946 ml (1 quart) of water
- 84 grams (3 ounces) of dried malt extract
- One packet of liquid yeast

1

Sanitize the bottle and cap it off with a piece of aluminum foil. Also, sanitize the rubber stopper and airlock. In a shallow pan boil the DME in the water for 10 minutes.

2

Cool the wort by placing the covered pan in ice water. Swab the mouth of the bottle with a ball of cotton soaked in alcohol.

3

Flame it with a lighter.

4

Pour in the wort.

5

Now add the yeast.

6

Seal the bottle with an airlock and stopper.

8

Remove the airlock and stopper, swab and flame any surfaces the starter may make contact with, and pour into the wort.

7

Aerate the bottle by agitating it for several minutes. Maintain temperatures between 18.3–23.9°C (65–75°F). Once active fermentation is apparent (12 hours or more) your starter is ready to pitch into the fermenter.

Ale creatures great and small (and some even lager!)

If yeast merely converted malt sugars into alcohol and CO_2, the brewing world would have less variety to offer. Indeed, many of the by-products of fermentation help define the distinct characteristics of certain beer styles. On the other hand, some by-products are less desirable, and can (sometimes literally) cause headaches. Here is a list of some of the organic compounds created, to varying degrees, during fermentation.

- **Aldehydes**–This group of acids causes a range of flavors, from a green-apple aroma to a flat flavor of "wet cardboard."
- **Esters**–This class of compounds produces fruity aromas. Some ales, such as the German weizen, depend on a small amount of esters to give the wheat beer its trademark banana aroma. Lager yeast produces far fewer esters than ale yeast.
- **Diacetyl**–Responsible for buttery or butterscotch aromas, diacetyl is more characteristic of ales than lagers. While its presence can be indicative of poor technique, some styles require a certain diacetyl flavor. Bock, for example, is a dark, rich lager that benefits from a slight buttery undertone.
- **Fusel Alcohols**–Ethyl alcohol defines the potency of beer, and is the desired product of fermentation. However, yeast also produce more complex alcohol compounds that can give beer a harsh bite and even cause slight headaches. Fusel alcohol is a naturally occurring compound that is generally produced early on in fermentation. Some homebrewers affix "blow-off" tubing on their primary fermenters in an attempt to expel this unpleasant compound. (See Chapter Four.)
- **Organic Acids**–Contaminated wort can result in high levels of these "goaty-flavored" substances.

Again, different strains of yeast ferment wort in different ways. By keeping your equipment sanitary, cooling your wort quickly, and choosing quality yeast suited to your targeted style, you'll easily control the perceptible levels of these and other by-products. If you feel you've met all of the above requirements and still make beer that is unsatisfactory, consult the troubleshooting tips.

Clean healthy yeast should produce great homebrew. The proliferation of quality liquid yeast strains has improved the quality and range of homebrew tremendously. There are yeast strains available for every type of beer, from the simplest ale to the most complex lambic. The key to good results is providing your yeast population with the right conditions, including temperature, handling, and propagation. Some high-gravity worts benefit from adding a yeast starter. This is not hard to do–it just requires a little extra time and cheap equipment. Never underestimate the role of yeast. Choosing a quality liquid strain that suits your particular style is as crucial as every other aspect of homebrewing. There are a number of companies that specialize in cultivating high-caliber yeast strains for just about every conceivable style of beer.

Water everywhere,
but what to drink?

IN CHAPTER THREE I explained that, for the extract brewer, the most important qualities of brew water are potability and taste. Water that is safe for consumption and free of off flavors and aromas is suitable for extract brewing.

The all-grain brewer may be more concerned with his or her water supply. Two additional characteristics that are important in all-grain brewing are pH level and ion content. The pH level refers to the acidic or alkaline nature of a liquid. The pH scale ranges from 1 (strongly acidic) to 14 (strongly alkaline) with 7 being neutral. Most water supplies hover around 7, though this can and does change among different municipal sources and can even fluctuate from season to season in a single water supply. Ions are electrically charged particles that influence chemical reactions in brewing and affect the flavor of finished beer. Ions may be a single atom or a group of atoms that attach to similar charges in water. All natural water contains ions. The ionic content of water and the relationship that various ions have with the brewing process is extremely complex, and I'm not going to explore the subject in great depth, here. It is not necessary for you to completely understand water chemistry to make great beer. However, if you are at the point where you are mashing a portion of your fermentables, it does help to have an understanding of some basic principles.

Now, you may be thinking: "If beer making began as a natural process, why do we need to concern ourselves with water chemistry?" For one, certain ions help to lower the pH of mash water, activating key starch-converting enzymes within the malt. Other ions increase the solvency of brew liquor, enabling it to dissolve and retain qualities from malt and hops. Ions–like copper and magnesium–in trace amounts, are a vital nutrient for yeast. Finally, some ions influence the flavor of finished beer by either accentuating characteristics of ingredients or lending tastes of their own.

▲ *You should not add mineral salts until you are sure that you understand the effect they will have on your brew.*

pH and brewing

The partial mash brewer usually adds grains to preheated water (65.6–70°C/ 150–58°F) for 45 minutes to an hour. This "single infusion" mash allows two major enzymes–alpha amylase, and to a lesser extent, beta amylase–to become active and convert long carbohydrate chains into maltriose, glucose, and other fermentable sugars. Just as certain temperatures are needed to activate and sustain enzyme activity, so too is a specific pH range. A mildly acidic mash (5·2–5·8) must be maintained for these enzymes to do their thing.

Luckily, many malts contain naturally acidic phosphates which lower the pH in the brewpot to proper levels. A highly alkaline water supply, however, may not come down to proper pH range by the mere addition of malt. Water that is high in bicarbonates (HCO_{3-1}) may require some treatment before it is suitable for brewing. We'll get back to this in a minute, but for now just realize that enzymes need mildly acidic conditions in which to work.

Ions and water

Expressed chemically, water is simply composed of two hydrogen atoms bound to a single oxygen atom. Like many compounds, water has a slight electrical charge: a partial positive from the hydrogen and a partial negative from the oxygen. These charges "seek" other molecules and atoms with similar charges to form bonds. Hence, table salt (Na+ Cl-) will dissolve in water because the positive sodium will bond with hydrogen and the negative chloride ion will bond with oxygen. All tap water and bottled spring or drinking water is rich with mineral ions.

Ions in water help to dissolve compounds that otherwise would fall out of solution. Calcium, for example, helps to dissolve resins and oils in hops. Distilled or "deionized" water would not be able to dissolve such compounds. Certain ions help to adjust the pH of water. Calcium and magnesium both help to make brew water more acidic. Brewers often add gypsum (calcium sulfate), calcium carbonate, epsom salts (magnesium sulfate), or other salts to lower mash pH.

Some ions have no chemical effect in brewing, but do contribute flavor characteristics. Small amounts of sodium give beer a smooth, rounded flavor. Sulfates paired with high levels of hop resins will give beer a harsh bitter taste. Such effects must be considered when treating brew liquor with salts.

Copper, magnesium, and zinc are vital yeast nutrients at trace levels. Since most water contains small amounts of these, you shouldn't try to add any more. All three are detrimental to your beer if present in excess.

pH

You can measure the pH of your water and your mash by using either paper test strips or a digital device. Test strips are cheaper but less accurate. These are dipped into a cool sample of liquid and held against a color chart to read pH. Digital meters can be dipped directly into the mash for a fast, precise readout.

Temporary and permanent hardness

When brewers speak of "hard" water, they are usually referring to the large amount of calcium and magnesium present. The term "temporary hardness" is used to describe water that is high in bicarbonates. However, water high in calcium and magnesium tends to be acidic, while water with excess bicarbonates is usually alkaline. Obviously, you want your water to be slightly acidic to promote a thorough starch conversion during the mash. Therefore, you won't want excessive levels of bicarbonate in your brew water. Besides raising the pH of the water, high levels of bicarbonate can promote the absorption of harsh hop flavors.

Unlike other ions, bicarbonates can be removed from your brew water by boiling and pouring the water off the precipitated minerals. If there are chalky deposits ringing the sink basins in your home, you can assume that your water has a high bicarbonate content.

Measuring the minerals

Ions are expressed in parts per million (ppm). This measurement is the same as the more easily applied milligrams per liter (mg/l). If you want to know the ionic content of your municipal supply, you can get a free analysis from your water company. Ask for the following information:

Calcium–Used to lower mash pH and accentuate hop flavors in beer. Look for levels of at least 50 ppm, but not over 100 ppm. An exception to this rule is the hard water of Burton upon Trent, which is used for brewing pale and India pale ales. There is as much as 295 ppm of calcium in these waters.

Carbonate/Bicarbonate–So-called "temporary hardness," this is often expressed as the total alkalinity of water. Keep levels under 50 ppm when brewing pale beers and 250 ppm when brewing dark beers.

Chloride–Low levels accentuate malt and hops characteristics. Higher levels give beer a rounded smooth flavor. Look for levels below 100 ppm.

Copper–Trace levels are a nutrient for yeast. Appreciable levels can be toxic to yeast.

Iron–Excessive amounts of iron will give your water, and hence your beer, a metallic, "blood-like" taste. Anything above a trace is undesirable.

Magnesium–Small amounts accentuate beer flavor, lower pH, and are a nutrient for yeast. At levels above 30 ppm, it can cause sharp, harsh flavors.

Sodium–At levels above 100 ppm, sodium can cause harsh flavors. At 50–100 ppm it can give beer a smooth, pleasant flavor.

Sulfate–Normally in the range of 10 ppm for pilsners to 70 ppm for ales.

Zinc–Anything above a trace in water to be used for brewing is undesirable.

Adjusting ion content

Adjusting the mineral content of water to duplicate a famous style of beer, bring out desired flavor, or to change pH can be tricky. Don't start dumping brewing salts in until you know the chemistry of your water and how the salts will interact. Common brewing salts: gypsum (calcium sulfate); calcium carbonate; epsom salts (magnesium sulfate); calcium chloride; non-iodized table salt (sodium chloride).

Conditioning your brew

Once your ale has finished fermenting, or your high-gravity ale or lager has matured, you may either bottle or keg. At this point your beer is beer, sans bubbles. A beer without bubbles is a beverage without sparkle, fizz, or a creamy aromatic head. To give your homebrew this final touch, you must carbonate it. The two methods are bottle or keg conditioning and forced carbonation. The former simply means that you add 70.8 grams (¾ cup) corn sugar (glucose) or 141.7 grams (1½ cups) DME (mainly maltose) to reactivate the yeast suspended in your 19-liter (5-gallon) batch of brew. Even though the yeast may be done fermenting the compounds provided by the malt, adding simple sugar will supply enough extra food for one last meal, causing the yeast to produce carbon dioxide, just the stuff you need to give your homebrew zing. By capping your bottles or securing the lid on your keg, the evolving gas will have nowhere to go except back into the beer. Give your primed and sealed brew two weeks to achieve desirable carbonation. If you are using bottles make sure they are brown, pop-top, and sturdy. I once poured some extra Irish stout into a cheap wine bottle for conditioning and ended up cleaning the walls of my closet. Quite a bit of CO_2 is created during bottle conditioning so be sure your bottles can take the pressure. Popular types of bottles include 355-ml (12-ounce), 650-ml (22-ounce), and 177.5-ml (6-ounce) "nip" bottles for high-potent homebrew. You can bottle in style and ease using bottles with a ceramic or plastic swing top. These are equipped with replaceable rubber washers that form a tight seal.

Forced carbonation requires the use of a CO_2 tank and regulator, and either a counterflow bottle filler (for bottling) or a soda keg with proper fittings. Forced bottle carbonation is a slow process that is far beyond my patience. Force-carbonating a keg, however, is easy and vivifying. Your brew will be carbonated in a few days and you'll even get a little exercise.

Bottling

MOST TYRO HOMEBREWERS bottle their beer. The reason for this is usually economics. Bottling requires little extra equipment, while kegging demands such pricey additions as a spare refrigerator, a keg and fittings, and a CO_2 tank and pressure regulator. All you need to bottle is some corn sugar, a short length of clear tubing, a bottle filler, a bottle capper, some caps, and, of course, bottles.

There are some advantages to bottling your beer. The first is portability. Bottles can be brought to parties, packed in picnic coolers, and given as gifts. If you come up with a particularly good recipe, bottles can be easily sent to competitions for evaluation. The main drawback to bottling is the time and effort it requires. Washing and sanitizing a couple dozen bottles and then filling and capping each one can test your forbearance. However, there are some steps that you can take that will cut down on the time and effort you spend bottling your homebrew.

Wash your bottles after each use

This sounds tedious, but a quick wash will save you a lot of future hassle. If you have a bottle washer, connect it to your sink before a tasting session. Decant your brew into your favorite glass and—with one eye on the creamy head and the other on the faucet—give your bottle a healthy blast of water. This will rid your bottle of the yeast sediment that would otherwise harden if left unattended.

Sanitize en masse

Properly cleaned bottles can be stored in a new plastic trashcan filled with cold water and a little household bleach. When it comes time to bottle, merely pluck the bottles

from the bin, give them a few rinses with hot water, and they are ready for use. You can even store sanitized bottles dry, by placing a piece of tin foil over the lip and placing them in a dry closet. If you use this method of soaking, try to find bottles without labels. You can either meticulously scrape the labels off used bottles or buy them bare at many homebrew supply shops. Finally, if you are storing your sanitizing container outside, be sure to cover it and mark it "NOT TRASH" in black indelible marker. You don't want the sanitation department to relieve you of your bottle supply.

Bottle 1-2-3

Some may tell you to spoon a little corn sugar into each bottle and then fill them with the beer. Ignore these people. For expedience and efficiency, you can't beat the old bottling bucket and solution of corn sugar. Many homebrew shops sell 19-liter (5-gallon) plastic fermenters intended to hold about 13.2 liters (3½ gallons) of fermenting brew. These make perfect bottling buckets. Boil 236 ml (½ pint) of water and 70.8 grams (¾ cup) corn sugar in a small saucepan or Pyrex glass container. Cover and leave to cool. Meanwhile, carefully siphon your beer into the bottling bucket. Remember, splashing introduces air,

which contains oxygen, which hastens deterioration of your beer. Once the bucket is full, gently pour in the corn-sugar mixture and stir using a sanitized, food-grade, plastic or stainless-steel spoon. Cover the bucket. Connect a bottle filler to some tubing, and the tubing to the spigot on the bucket (all of which have been sanitized, of course). Soak your bottle caps in a dilute bleach-water solution for about 20 minutes. Boiling caps is a bad idea, as the heat can damage the inner seal.

▲ *A quick rinse with a bottle washer right after you pour your beer will save time and work in the future.*

Now, line your bottles up and begin filling. Fill to the rim and pull out the bottle filler. This should leave a little desirable space around the neck. Place a cap over the top and move on to the next bottle. When all bottles are filled, crimp the caps and mark them for identification. Store your bottles in the same dark, quiet place you stored your fermenter.

Most ale will be ready for consumption within two weeks. Certain higher-gravity ales, like imperial stout and barley wine, will greatly benefit from prolonged aging in the bottle.

Soothing the savage yeast

Any unfiltered beer will have some yeast left in suspension. This is normal. If you find that the flavor of your beer is dominated by a yeasty taste, there are a few steps you can take. First, try adding a fining agent like gelatin or isinglass before you bottle. This will help drop the yeast out of suspension. There will still be enough to facilitate carbonation, but the ranks will be culled to a level better suiting your taste. Second, always store your bottles upright, and don't shake or handle them roughly. You want to keep the sediment at the bottom of the bottle, away from your beer. When you pour a glass, stop just before the sediment reaches the lip of the bottle. Now, go to the faucet and rinse.

Kegging

AS WE SAW EARLIER, there are a number of clever devices that allow you to keg a small volume of beer. By far, the most convenient, reliable, and enduring is the employment of a used 19-liter (5-gallon) soda keg. These are designed to store soft-drink syrup, which is then mixed with water and carbon dioxide. These kegs are being phased out in favor of plastic bags set inside cardboard boxes. Scavengers that we are, homebrewers have found that the metal canisters can be bought used and rigged to hold and dispense beer. Soda kegs have the added benefits of allowing quick-force carbonation, and doubling as a lagering vessel. A complete kegging system requires a spare refrigerator, CO_2 tank and regulator, proper fittings, hoses, and a tap.

Depending on where you live and what equipment your area homebrew supply shop stocks, you will come across various devices designed to hold your beer. Some shops sell the Party Pig®, a handy, inexpensive vessel built to hold a portion of your brew. You may also find access to small barrel-shaped kegs that use seltzer cartridges to maintain carbonation and dispense homebrew. There are a number of options on the market. The girth of your wallet may dictate which system you decide to choose.

Inevitably, every homebrewer considers kegging as an alternative to bottling. Kegging takes less time, gives you the option to force-carbonate, and holds a certain appeal that can be best described as just being "cool." There's something about bellying up to your own bar, grabbing the wooden tap handle, and pouring a pint of your latest batch of brew. Gatherings become parties.

▼ *Basic soda keg setup.*

The key to successful kegging is maintenance of your equipment. Most used soda kegs have spent years squirting out soft-drink syrup. Consequently, the internal and external parts will need cleaning and/or replacing. The following parts need to be inspected: inlet and outlet valves and rubber O-rings, the rubber gasket around the lid, the liquid and gas dip tubes and O-rings, and the interior of the keg. New parts are easy to come by, whether at your local shop or through mail-order companies. Old, malfunctioning parts or broken O-rings will cause leaks, making it impossible to properly carbonate your beer, keep oxygen out, and maintain pressure. Clean your keg with B-Brite, TSP, or Iphodor solution. Never use bleach on stainless steel.

For all practical purposes, consider your keg one big bottle. If you plan to carbonate your beer using corn sugar or DME, follow the instructions for bottling, but use about a third less priming agent. When the keg is filled, secure the lid and add some CO_2 pressure. Listen for leaks. If you hear any hissing, release the pressure and readjust the lid. Once you are sure of a proper seal, apply a small amount of CO_2 pressure and pull the purge pin to allow air to escape. This will be replaced by the incoming CO_2, discouraging oxidation. Store your brew at appropriate temperatures for a couple of weeks.

CHAPTER SEVEN

Charts and Worksheets

Homebrew charts and worksheets

THE INTERMEDIATE WORKSHEETS are designed to help you make great homebrew! Using these aids in conjunction with other information in this book, you will gain a better understanding of how each homebrew recipe ingredient affects your beer; organize all needed recipe and procedural information in one accessible area (no frantic mid-brew page flipping); evaluate your efforts; and keep all those great batch sessions filed for later reference. As your homebrew knowledge increases, you can even create your own recipes designed to your personal taste specifications.

The worksheets are divided into four sections: **Homebrew Recipe/Worksheet**; **Homebrew Flowchart: Hot Side**; **Homebrew Flowchart: Cold Side**; and **Homebrew Results/Journal**. Each of these sections will be filled out, to some extent, before you start to brew. Doing this will constrain all the information you need to just a few pages, freeing you to concentrate on brewing your excellent beer! I'll show you how to use each of these four sections in a minute, but first let's take a quick look at each.

Homebrew Recipe/Worksheet

This section is subdivided into five parts: **Basic information**; **Homebrew Recipe**; **Ingredient Characteristics Breakdown**; **Target Homebrew Characteristics**; and **Equipment/Procedural Notes**.

Basic information is just that: name of beer, volume brewed, style, and so on.

In the **Homebrew Recipe** space, you'll enter the recipe of the beer you're going to brew, whether from this book or another.

The **Ingredient Characteristics Breakdown** table is designed for the home-brewer who wishes to understand how each ingredient affects the characteristics of his or her final brew. By listing all of the added malt, hops, yeast, etc., you can estimate how each contributes its unique quality to the given style of beer. Use the **Ingredient Profile Tables** in the back of the book to obtain the needed information, or, for more current statistics, use the specifications often supplied on the packaging of your malt, hops, and yeast. Once you have entered this data, use the **Calculations Tables** to obtain utilization estimates. While these are admittedly tentative pre-dictions, comparing your goals with your outcome will give you some idea about the efficiency of your system, allowing for adjustments in procedure and experimentation with different equipment and ingredients.

Imagine exploring a dark cave and, once deep inside its winding labyrinth, you suddenly realize you forgot to tie a lead rope at the entrance. You'd be lost! Wise spelunkers checklist all of their tools before taking the plunge, and as a brewer you should list all of your tools in the **Equipment Procedural Notes** section. Making sure all needed equipment is sanitized and ready for use will save time and needless worry. The only thing you should be rushing for mid-brew is another glass of your latest homebrew. Also, variations in equipment can have an effect on the efficiency of your system. Recording the tools of your trade will serve as reason and reminder to step up the quality of your equipment.

In the **Procedural** column you can transfer the recipe instructions, or, if you're brewing an original, you can outline your own game plan.

Homebrew Flowchart: hot side–cold side

You'll be filling out most parts of these two tables *before* you start brewing. Space is allotted for you to enter ingredients used and when you'll be adding them. This serves as a procedural flowchart. All that will be left for you to do while brewing is to check off each step as it is completed, and record any observations and/or incidentals as necessary. This is where it all happens and these charts will guide you through the whole process, from boil to bottle.

Homebrew Results/Journal

This section allows you to compare your results with your goals. Is your IPA properly hoppy? Did you hit the right color on that last Pilsner? By comparing your results with your predictions, you'll gain an understanding of the effectiveness of your system and, perhaps, a new-found respect for all the complex variables involved in the creation of homebrew.

In the Notes area, you can offer possible reasons for why your beer hit or missed your target and plan changes in equipment and procedure for future batches. Of course, your primary concern should be whether or not your brew is tasty and drinkable. Don't let missed theoretical targets discourage you. Even the masters admit that predictions are difficult. First enjoy what you've made, then consider what might be done to come closer to the mark next time around. Remember that you are the artist and your palette is as unique as your palate.

Filling out the homebrew recipe worksheets

THE EASIEST WAY TO learn how to use these worksheets is by example. So let's fill one out together. Note: I've completed the worksheets as if the batch had already been brewed, to fully illustrate how each section works.

Say you're working with the following recipe:

Theo's Theoretical Ale

OG:1·016   FG: 1·014   HCU: 19   IBUs: 52   Boil Time: 1 hour

8 oz crystal malt
1 lb pale malt
3⅓ lb amber malt extract
3⅓ lb light malt extract
½ tsp gypsum
2 oz Northern Brewer hops
1½ oz Cascade hops
1 tsp Irish moss
1 package Wyeast 1056 American ale yeast
¾ cup corn sugar (for priming)

METHOD
- Heat 3–4 gallons of water to 155°F. Add crystal and pale malts and let steep for 30–35 minutes, maintaining above temperature. Scoop out grains and sparge with 165°F water. Remove pot from heat and add gypsum and malt extracts. When you are sure that all of the extract is dissolved, return pot to heat and bring to a boil. Add 1 oz Northern Brewer hops. Stir and watch pot for boil-overs. After 30 minutes, add the rest of the Northern Brewer hops. After 10 minutes, add Irish moss. Add 1 oz Cascade hops during last 5 minutes of boil.
- Cool wort to about 75°F and siphon or strain into primary fermenter. Add cold water to bring wort up to 5-gallon mark. Pitch yeast at 65–70°F. Ferment at 65°F for 4–7 days or until apparent fermentation has ceased.
- Rack to secondary and add ½ oz Cascade hops. Store as before for two weeks. Prime with corn sugar and bottle or keg. Let beer carbonate and further age for one to two weeks.

First enter your basic information:

Name of Beer: *Theo's theo ale*
Date Brewed: *1/24/98*
Description: *amber, med. body,*
 hoppy ale

Vol. Brewed: *5 gallons*
Style: *IPA*
Time Preboil/Boil: *30–35 min 60 min*

Next, transfer the recipe to the Homebrew Recipe table. To avoid being redundant and possibly insulting to your intelligence, I've omitted this step. I will, however, suggest that you include the forms of ingredients you'll be using (e.g. pellet hops as opposed to whole hops) as these may have some effect on how they are utilized in the brewpot and fermenter.

Using the tables from the back of the book, fill out the characteristics of each ingredient, as follows:

INGREDIENT CHARACTERISTICS BREAKDOWN

Key: G = Gravity; °L = Degrees Lovibond; α% = AA%; TIME = Time Spent in Boil; U = decimal utilization; ATTN% = Attenuation

MALT/ADJ	LBS.	G	°L	HOPS	OZ	α%	TIME	U	M/C	YEAST	ATTN%
Crystal	0·5	25	40	NB	1	11	60 min	25	Gyp	W1056	73–77
Pale 2 Row	1	30	4	NB	1	11	30 min	10	IrM		
AbME	3·3	35	50	Casc	1	5	5 min	0			
LiME	3·3	30	5	Casc	0·5	5	Dry	0			

◄ *Note that these numbers are based on manufacturer's specifications, not on the data provided in the ingredients chart.*

Note that pounds of malt and ounces of hops should be entered as decimals, gravity as a whole number (25 as opposed to 1·025), and that hops should be itemized according to the total time spent in the boil.

Using the calculations tables in the back of this book, you can now make final predictions based on the information entered in the above table. Depending on the amount of procedural factors you wish to take into account, your calculations can be as simple or as complex as you desire.

TARGET HOMEBREW CHARACTERISTICS

OG: 1·056   FG: 1·014   HCU: 19   IBU: 52   Other: Clearly hoppy!!

As we saw earlier, your predictions take into account some, but not all, of the factors involved in the transition of characteristics from ingredient to final brew. The quality of your homebrew equipment can affect your procedure and, therefore, the accuracy of your results. For example, the addition of an immersion wort chiller to your system greatly decreases the time it takes to cool your pot of goodness. Any excessive time the wort spends hovering between 60°C (140°F) and 26.7°C (80°F) opens a window of opportunity for wild yeast and bacteria to settle and develop in your brewpot. This can be detrimental to all aspects of your beer. Make a note of the cooling method you're using and consider upgrading if you're not getting desired results. By recording all of your equipment, you can further refine your system by noting changes in quality and accuracy as you upgrade your home brewery.

EQUIPMENT/PROCEDURAL NOTES

6·7 gal. plastic fermenter (for primary)	All steps fit into Flowcharts
5 gal. glass carboy (for aging)	
5 gal. brewpot	
Triple-scale hydrometer	
Floating thermometer	
Bleach (as sanitizer)	
Bottle washer (just bought it!)	
Muslin and grain bags (for grains and hops)	
Plastic tubing (for transfers and cooling siphon)	
Measuring cup and spoons	
1 gal. water for sparging	
Spray bottle	
Heat source: electric range	Cooling method: single-basin system

◄ *While the purpose of the flowcharts is to organize the recipe instructions in a chronological format, there are sometimes steps that cannot be readily entered into the flowcharts. You should highlight any such steps in the Procedural Notes section.*

Now enter ingredients and procedural information into the flowcharts:

HOMEBREW FLOWCHART: HOT SIDE
PRE-BOIL

I Grains Crystal Malt Pale Malt		II Malt Extracts Amber Malt Extract Light Malt Extract		III Adjuncts None		IV Brew Salts Gypsum	
1) Time Added: At 68.3°C (155°F)	✗	1) Time Added: After 1 remove and Sparge the Grains	✗	1) Time Added:		1) Time Added: Along with the Extracts	✗
Temp Added: Same as above	✗			2) Time Added:	✗	Amount Added: ½ tsp	✗
2) Time Removed: After 30–35 min.	✗					2) Time Added:	
Temp Removed: Same as above	✗					Amount Added:	
NOTES		**NOTES**		**NOTES**		**NOTES**	
It's pretty tough to regulate temp on an electric range. Gotta think about getting a gas burner.		Glad I warmed the extracts before trying to pour them in. That's some thick syrup!				No problems here. Hopefully this will lower the pH of my water so that more bitterness can be extracted from my hops.	

BOIL

V Boiling Hops 1 oz Northern Brewer 1 oz Northern Brewer		VI Clarifiers Irish Moss		VII Finishing hops 1 oz Cascade Hops 0·5 oz Cascade Hops	
1) Time(s)	Amount(s)	1) Time(s)	Amount(s)	1) Time(s)	Amount(s)
60 min	1 oz ✗	20 min	1 tsp ✗	5 min	1 oz ✗
30 min	1 oz ✗			Dry	0·5 oz ✗
NOTES		**NOTES**		**NOTES**	
As soon as I added those first hops, the pot started foaming up. Luckily I had that spray bottle to avoid a boil-over.		Stirred it in and let it do its thing.		I love the smell of these hops. Maybe next time I'll put them in loose. It might help release more of those great oils.	

Note that when you enter the times you're adding the ingredients, you should do so in relation to the total time of the boil. Here, the first additions of the Northern Brewer hops are dropped at the beginning of the boil, or the 60-minute mark. The next ounce of Northern Brewer hops is added at the 30-minute mark. This means they will spend 30 minutes in the boil. The ounce of Cascade Hops is introduced 55 minutes into the 60-minute boil, so enter 5 minutes as the total time spent in the wort. Working with a timer that counts down from 60 minutes, you simply add these ingredients when the corresponding times are reached.

Homebrew flowchart: cold side

COOLING/PITCHING

VIII Cooling	IX Pitching Yeast: 1056 Wyeast Liquid
1) Time wort removed from heat: 12.35 pm	1) Temp yeast pitched: 21.1°C (70°F)
2) Took How Long to Cool?: 2 Hours!!	2) Amount pitched: One packet
NOTES	**NOTES**
Man, that took a long time to cool. I need to find a way to get this stuff down to pitching temp. more quickly!	Made sure I sanitized and rinsed the mouth of the packet before I put in the wort. Also, I gently stirred it in with a sanitized plastic spoon. The transfer went pretty well. Only lost a little beer when the hose slipped out of the fermenter.

Here you want to record the specific time that the wort is removed from the heat, so you can time duration between near-boiling and pitching temperature.

FERMENTING/AGING

X Primary Fermentation	XI Aging
1) Vessel: 6·7 gal. plastic fermenter	1) Date racked: 01/29/98
2) Ambient Temp: About 23.9°C (75°F)	
3) Date/Time started fermenting: 10:30 pm, 1/24/98	3) Dry hops: Cascade Form: Pellets Amount: 0·5 oz
4) Date fermentation ceased: 1/29/98	4) Ambient Temp: About 23.9°C (75°F)
NOTES	**NOTES**
Pretty vigorous fermentation! Kept the wort cool by draping a wet T-shirt over it.	Decided to dry-hop loose and siphon the beer off later. There was a little splashing during transfer, but not too much. That beer already smells good!

PRIMING/BOTTLING

XII Priming/Bottling				
1) Priming agent: Corn sugar	Amount: ¾ cup	2) Bottled **✗**	Kegged	Other
3) Ambient storage temp: 23.9°C (75°F)		Stored How Long? Tried the first after a week. Let the rest age for the full two weeks		
NOTES				
Let age for two weeks in secondary. Wow, the beer really cleared up and actually darkened a little by the time it was ready to bottle. Primed with corn sugar, stirring it in with a sanitized plastic spoon. Bottling was crazy! I was trying to watch the siphon intake at the carboy and the filling of each bottle at the same time. The only way I could stop the flow of beer was by pinching the end of the siphon tube. What a mess! I need to get one of those plastic bottle fillers and maybe even a plastic racking cane. Maybe I'll get a bottling bucket and siphon into that first. When all was through, I had lost about 16 oz of precious brew to spillage. The capper worked great and was actually kinda fun!				

Homebrew Results/Journal

RESULTS

Predicted OG: 1·056	Actual OG: 1·052	Predicted FG: 1·014	Actual FG: 1·014	Alcohol:
Calculated IBU: 57	Perceived bitterness: nice bitterness and wonderful floral aroma			
Calculated HCU: 19	Resultant color: deep amber color, looks great through the light			
Desired aroma/flavor From hops: that distinctive citrusy Cascade quality	Perceived aroma/flavor: wasn't let down, but I may dry-hop with a full ounce next time			
Desired malt flavors: full malt flavor	Perceived malt flavors: nice body, a little thin in the middle, but a distinct warming finish			
Desired body: medium	Resultant body: pretty good, just a bit watery. Might have to do with the sparging technique			
Off/odd flavors: just a hint of cider at the edges. Not perfect, but it won't slow me down!				
Overall impression: pretty good IPA.				
NOTES/IMPRESSIONS/FUTURE GOALS				
Changes I'll Make Next Time Around: 1) Sparge a little more thoroughly 2) Drop in hops loose and remove through filtered siphoning 3) Get or make an immersion wort chiller! 4) Buy a racking cane and bottle filler 5) Primary-ferment in a 6 gallon glass carboy with blow-off tube				

Here is where you match goals with reality. Be honest or you won't know how you can improve, but don't be too hard on yourself if things don't turn out perfect. Remember, you made it, so appreciate what went right, and try to build on that.

CHAPTER EIGHT

Explore and Appreciate

Recipes

THE FOLLOWING ARE some intermediate recipes culled from homebrew supply shops across the country. These recipes are a little more complex than the recipe in Chapter Two. Some are partial mash, others require the preparation of a yeast starter, and I've even thrown in a few lagers. Where possible, I've included original gravity, final gravity, and bitterness. Keep in mind that these numbers were arrived at empirically by the designers of the recipes. When you do your own calculations, you may arrive at numbers that are slightly higher. This is because calculations assume 100% efficiency. By comparing your calculations to the numbers in the recipes, and then to your own, you'll get an idea of the efficiency of your own system.

I have also included, in quotes, any informative notes that were given to me by the recipe designers. Any observations or information not in quotes are my additions.

▼ *Beer can be an excellent partner to many foods.*

Ales

M a i d e n ' s   D r e a m

Alfred's Brewing Supply

"Maiden's Dream is extra light in color and taste with a bold hop flavor. The Maiden is a summer hit with all!"

OG: 1·045   FG: 1·006
ABV: 5%   IBU: 21·5   SRM: 2·0

227 g (½ lb) pale malted grain
227 g (½ lb) pale crystal malted grain
1 tsp gypsum
14 g (½ oz) Chinook fresh hops (6·5HBU)
1.36 kg (3 lb) Dutch dry malt extract extra light
908 g (2 lb) dry rice syrup solids
14 g (½ oz) Hallertau fresh hops (2HBU)
14 g (½ oz) Saaz fresh hops (2HBU)
Liquid yeast (American Ale)
70.8 g (¾ cup) corn sugar (priming)

M E T H O D

- Crack grain, place with gypsum in 5.6 liters (1½ gallons) cold water. Heat to boil, remove grain and discard. Add Chinook hops, boil 40 minutes. Remove hops. Add malt extract, boil 10 minutes. Add Hallertau and Saaz hops, boil 2 minutes. Sparge into fermenter and add cold water to 19 liters (5 gallons). When below 23.9°C (75°F), add prepared liquid yeast.
- Ferment for 4 days at 21.1°C (70°F), rack to secondary fermenter for 14 days. Rack to bottling bucket, add priming sugar and bottle.

Belgian Wit Ale

Chris Russell, New York Homebrew, Inc.

Chris's verdict: "This is the ultimate beer to make for special occasions! This beer should be cloudy and even have a white opalescence."

5 gallons partial mash/extract
OG: 1·045   ABV: 4·5%   IBUs: 10

227 g (½ lb) unmalted wheat
227 g (½ lb) flaked oats
1.81 kg (4 lb) Alexander's Wheat Syrup
908 g (2 lb) Weyermann Pilsner
454 g (1 lb) wheat malt
21 g (¾ oz) Crystal or Saaz hops (3% alpha)
7 g (¼ oz) Crystal or Saaz hops
454 g (1 lb) light raw honey
7 g (¼ oz) coriander seed (fine crush)
9.3 g (⅓ oz) curaçao (bitter) orange peel (chopped)
½ tsp dried ginger or 1½ tsp fresh ginger
½ tsp crushed cardamom
Wyeast #3942 or #3944 – 946.3 ml (1 quart) yeast starter prepared

METHOD

- Crack grains–tie up in muslin bags.
- Steep grains between 65.6–68.35°C (150–55°F) for 60–75 minutes.
- Raise mash to 75.58°C (168°F)–shut off heat.
- Remove grains–add extract.
- Bring to boil–add 21 g (0·75 oz) of Crystal or Saaz hops.
- Boil 40 minutes–add 7 g (0·25 oz) of Crystal or Saaz hops.
- Boil 10 minutes–add the raw light honey.
- Boil 5 minutes–add the coriander, orange peel, ginger, and cardamom.
- Boil 5 more minutes–total boiling time: 60 minutes.
- Shut off heat–steep for 10 minutes.
- Chill to 18.3°C (65°F) ASAP.
- Transfer wort to primary fermenter.
- Aerate well–pitch yeast.
- Ferment at 15.6–18.3°C (60–65°F).
- No secondary fermenter used.
- Either bottle or keg and enjoy!

Warm Weather Wheat (Hefe-weizen)

Peter A'Hearn, Homebrew Mart

Peter's verdict: "Ah, warm weather and our thoughts turn to beaches, bare legs, and Hefe-weizen! The dry extract gives a lighter color and crisper finish than the liquid. The Cascade hops are untraditional, but give the beer zing."

2.72 kg (6 lb) dry wheat extract
28.35 g (1 oz) Cascade hops (5·4% alpha)
28.35 g (1 oz) Cascade hops
White Labs Hefe-weizen yeast
70.87 grams (¾ cup) corn sugar (priming)

METHOD

- Add dry wheat extract to 7.57–11.355 liters (2–3 gallons) water.
- Bring to boil, stirring in the extract.
- Once hot break has subsided, add 28.35 g (1 oz) Cascade hops. Boil 55 minutes.
- Add 28.35 g (1 oz) Cascade hops.
- Boil 5 minutes–shut off heat.
- Chill wort to 21.1–23.9°C (70–75°F).
- Transfer wort to primary fermenter.
- Top off to 19 liters (5 gallons) with cold sanitized water. Aerate well–pitch yeast.
- Primary-ferment for about 7 days.
- Transfer to secondary fermenter, and ferment for 7 days.
- Bottle, using 70.87 g (¾ cup) corn sugar.
- Age in bottle 7 to 10 days.

Aloha Pale Ale

Marci, Maui Home Brew Supply

This is a good American-style pale ale that can be "Hawaiianized" by adding tropical fruits before or at bottling.

OG: 1·050   IBUs: 30

454 g (1 lb) crystal malt (20 L)
3.18 kg (7 lb) pale malt extract
28.35 g (1 oz) Northern Brewer hops
1 tsp Irish moss
14 g (½ oz) Cascade hops
1 pkg Edme dry yeast
70.87 g (¾ cup) corn sugar (priming)

METHOD

- Place crushed grains in pot and cover with water. Heat to 65.6°C (150°F), and hold at that temperature for 30 minutes. Turn off heat and let stand for 15 minutes.
- Pour the grain into a strainer above your brew kettle.
- Sparge until run-off becomes clear. Discard the grain.
- Add the malt extract and more water, if needed, until your pot is ¾ full. Stir, occasionally.
- Add Northern Brewer hops and boil for 60 minutes. Continue stirring to keep syrup from sticking to the bottom of your pot.
- With 15 minutes left, add the Irish moss.
- With 5 minutes left, add Cascade hops.
- Boil for the final five minutes and remove kettle from stove.
- Place lid over kettle and cool wort as quickly as possible.
- Pour wort through a sanitized strainer into your sanitized primary fermenter. Add water (previously boiled and cooled) to equal 19 liters (5 gallons). Cover immediately.
- Prepare a yeast slurry.
- When wort is below 26.7°C (80°F), stir in slurry. Make sure the lid (or rubber stopper) and airlock are airtight.
- Ferment at approximately 21.1°C (70°F) until fermentation is complete (usually 5–7 days).
- Rack into a secondary for 10–14 days.

- Transfer to a bottling bucket and bottle using 70.87 grams (¾ cup) corn sugar.
- OPTIONAL: Add fruits to bottling bucket or individual bottles. Make sure the fruit is sanitary. I like to add raspberry to part of the batch and mango to part of the batch.
- Or, just drink it as it is. Aloha, and enjoy!

El Niño Red

Lynne O'Conner,
St Patrick's of Texas
Brewing Supply

57 g (⅛ lb) chocolate malt
454 g (1 lb) Czech Crystal (50 L)
454 g (1 lb) Czech Pilsner
454 g (1 lb) Czech Munich
2.72 kg (6 lb) pale malt syrup extract
42.52 g (1·5 oz) Challenger hops for bittering
28.35 g (1 oz) Golding hops for flavoring
28.35 g (1 oz) Golding hops for aroma
#1084 Wyeast Irish Ale yeast
70.87 g (¾ cup) corn sugar (priming)

METHOD

- Add grains to 2.8 liters (¾ gallon) of water and raise temperature to 65.6–70°C (150–58°F).
- Remove from heat, cover, leave for 40 minutes.
- Dump contents of pot into a colander or large strainer and catch the running liquid in a pot.
- Sparge with 1.9 liters (½ gallon) of 76.7°C (170°F) water and catch this run-off as well. Discard grains.
- Stir in extract, until it is completely dissolved. (Add more water if necessary.)
- Bring to a boil. When hot break subsides, add Challenger hops.
- With 10 minutes left, add 28.3 grams (1 oz) Golding hops.
- With 1 minute left, add 28.3 grams (1 oz) Golding hops. Remove from heat and quickly cool.
- Pitch with prepared yeast packet and primary-ferment for 6–8 days.
- Rack to secondary and store for an additional 7–10 days.
- Bottle using 70.8 grams (¾ cup) priming sugar.

Scottish Ale

Jim McHale, Beer Unlimited

OG: 1·048   FG: 1·020   ABV: 4·13%

Wyeast 1728 Scottish Ale Yeast
227 g (½ lb) Munton's Crystal
57 g (⅛ lb) black barley
57 g (⅛ lb) roasted barley
1 can John Bull Light (unhopped)
1.3 kg (3 lb) Laaglander Extra Dry Malt Extract
28.3 g (1 oz) East Kent Goldings hops (6·7% alpha)
1 tsp Irish moss (optional)
47.2 g (½ cup) corn sugar (priming)

METHOD

- For best results, pop the Wyeast packet 48 hours before brew day.
- Make a yeast starter 24 hours before brew day.
- Steep grains until water begins to boil. Return to boil.
- Turn off heat and stir in extracts. Return to boil.
- When boiling starts, add 28.3 g (1 oz) East Kent Goldings. Boil for 60 minutes.
- Add Irish moss for last 30 minutes.
- Pitch yeast when wort cools.
- Primary-ferment for 7–10 days or until finished.
- Bottle with priming sugar and condition 2–4 weeks.

Hoppy Gurkha's IPA

Peter A'Hearn, Home Brew Mart

Peter's verdict: "This is a more traditional IPA than many you have tried. It has the high hop levels of an American IPA, but uses English hops, sugar, water with a high salt content, and an English ale yeast to produce a more traditional beer."

227 g (½ lb) Crystal malt (40 L)
227 g (½ lb) carapils
2 tsp gypsum
3.63 kg (8 lb) pale malt extract
454 g (1 lb) golden brown sugar
42.5 g (1½ oz) Northdown hops (8% alpha)
28.3 g (1 oz) Fuggles hops (4·2% alpha)
White Labs English Ale Yeast
28.3 g (1 oz) First Gold hops
70.8 g (¾ cup) corn sugar (priming)

METHOD

- Add grains and gypsum to 1.8 liters (½ gallon) of water.
- Raise temperature to about 68.3°C (155°F), and hold for 45 minutes.
- Sparge into brewpot.
- Add extract and brown sugar plus water to bring brewpot about ¾ full.
- Bring to boil. When hot break subsides, add Northdown hops.
- With 15 minutes left, add Fuggles.
- After 60 minutes have expired, remove pot from heat and cool.
- Pitch yeast.
- Ferment for 6–8 days, or until bubbling has all but ceased.
- Rack into secondary and add First Gold hops.
- Store for at least 5 more days, and bottle using 70.8 grams (¾ cup) corn sugar.
- Store an additional 10–14 days. Enjoy!

Dry Stout

Jim McHale, Beer Unlimited

OG: 1·052   FG: 1·014   ABV: 4·90%

Pitchable English ale yeast
454 g (1 lb) roasted barley
454 g (1 lb) black barley (not Black Patent)
1 can John Bull Dark
1 can Munton's Dark
1 can Alexander's Pale Kicker
56.7 g (2 oz) East Kent Goldings hops
1 tsp Irish moss
28.35 g (1 oz) Challenger hops
70.87 g (¾ cup) corn sugar (priming)

METHOD

- Remove pitchable yeast from the refrigerator. No other preparation is necessary with pitchable yeast.
- Steep grains until water begins to boil. Remove grains.
- Turn off heat and stir in extracts. Return to boil.
- When boil starts, add 56.7 g (2 oz) East Kent Golding hops. Boil for 60 minutes.
- Add Irish moss for last 30 minutes.
- Add 14 g (½ oz) Challenger hops for last 15 minutes.
- Add 14 g (½ oz) Challenger hops for last 2 minutes.
- Cool wort quickly and pitch yeast.
- Primary-ferment for 5–8 days or until complete.
- Rack to secondary for an additional 5 days.
- Prime with 70.8 g (¾ cup) corn sugar and bottle. Enjoy!

Porter

Jim McHale, Beer Unlimited

OG: 1·050   FG: 1·016   ABV: 4·39%

This particular recipe took first place in the 1997 War of the Worts competition. If your local supplier doesn't carry the specific ingredients, ask him for substitutes.

Wyeast #1084 Irish Ale Yeast
227 g (½ lb) American crystal malt (40 L)
227 g (½ lb) chocolate malt
114 g (¼ lb) black malt
2 boxes Northwestern Amber
1 Alexander's Pale Kicker
28.3 g (1 oz) Nugget hops
1 tsp Irish moss (optional)
57 g (2 oz) Willamette hops
70.8 g (¾ cup) corn sugar (priming)

METHOD

- Pop the yeast packet 48 hours before brew day.
- Prepare a yeast starter 24 hours before brew day.
- Steep grains until water begins to boil. Remove grains.
- Turn off heat and stir in extracts. Return to boil.
- When boiling starts, add 28.3 g (1 oz) Nugget hops. Boil for 60 minutes.
- Add Irish moss (optional) for last 30 minutes.
- Add 28.3 g (1 oz) Willamette hops for last 2 minutes.
- Cool wort quickly, and pitch yeast starter.
- Primary-ferment for 7–10 days.
- Dry-hop with the final ounce of Willamette. (Add hops to primary fermenter two days before racking.)
- Rack to secondary for an additional 7 days.
- Bottle with 70.8 g (¾ cup) priming sugar.
- Store bottles for a week or two. Enjoy!

Lagers

Bohemian Pilsner

Jim McHale, Beer Unlimited

OG: 1·048   FG: 1·012   ABV: 4·64%

Wyeast #2278 Czech Pils lager yeast
1 can Alexander's Pale
1.3 kg (3 lb) Laaglander Extra Light Dry Malt Extract
10 HBU Saaz (bittering), plus
1 tsp Irish moss
57 g (2 oz) Saaz (flavor and aroma)
1 tbsp gelatin
70.8 g (¾ cup) corn sugar (priming)

METHOD
- Pop yeast packet 48 days before brew day.
- Prepare yeast starter 24 hours before brew day.
- Bring water to boil. Turn off the heat and stir in extracts. Return to boil.
- When boiling starts add bittering Saaz. Boil for 60 minutes total.
- Add Irish moss for the last 30 minutes.
- Add 14 g (½ oz) Saaz hops for the last 15 minutes.
- Add14 g (½ oz) Saaz hops for the last 5 minutes.
- Cool wort quickly and pitch yeast starter.
- Primary-ferment at 10°C (50°F) for 10–14 days.
- Rack to secondary. Dry-hop with 28.3 g (1 oz) Saaz hops.
- Lager for 4–6 weeks at 4.4–7.2°C (40–45°F).
- Add gelatin two days before bottling.
- Bottle with priming sugar and store cool for as long as you can stand (varies with individual). Drink and enjoy!

Doppelbock

Chris Russell, New York Homebrew, Inc.

Chris's verdict: "This recipe is fairly simple to put together, but since it is a true partial mash and may even be your first attempt at a lager, I have written out a short set of special instructions (detailed below) to keep in mind. Happy brewing!"

OG: 1·068   ABV: 6%   IBUs: 24

340 g (¾ lb) Belgian Special "B"
114 g (¼ lb) German Carafe
2.9 kg (6½ lb) Ireks Amber Extract
681 g (1½ lb) Dark Munich
21 g (¾ oz) Perle hops
14 g (½ oz) German Hallertau
Wyeast #2308 lager–1 quart yeast starter, prepared

METHOD
- Crack grains, tie up in muslin bags.
- Steep at 66.7–68.9°C (152–56°F) for 45 minutes.
- Raise mash to 75.6°C (168°F). Turn off heat.
- Remove grains and stir in extracts. Return to boil.
- When boiling, add Perle hops.
- Boil 50 minutes, add Hallertau hops.
- Boil 10 more minutes–total boiling time is 60 minutes. Turn off heat. Cool wort to 18.3°C (65°F), ASAP.
- Aerate wort well and pitch yeast starter.
- Primary-ferment at 12.8–15.6°C (55–60°F).
- Rack to secondary fermenter. Maintain secondary at approximately 4.4°C (40°F) for 1 month. Either bottle or keg.

Hybrid styles

California Common

Lisa Huddock
Beer Unlimited

Lisa's verdict: "Everyone who brews this style tries to copy Anchor Steam, the standard for the style. This is a different kind of California Common than Anchor–especially with the hop schedule. Let's call it California Un-common."

OG: 1·045   FG: 1·008
ABV: 4·77%

Wyeast #2112 California lager yeast
227 g (½ lb) German CaraMunich II
2 boxes Northwestern Gold
28.3 g (1 oz) Chinook hops
1 tsp Irish moss
14 g (½ oz) Hallertau Hersbrucker hops
28.3 g (1 oz) Northern Brewer hops
70.8 g (¾ cup) corn sugar (priming)

METHOD

- Pop yeast packet 48 days before brew day.
- Prepare yeast starter 24 hours before brew day.
- Steep grains until water begins to boil. Remove grains.
- Remove from heat and stir in Northwestern extract.
- Return to boil.
- When boil recommences add 14 g (½ oz) Chinook hops. This will be boiled for the full 60 minutes.
- Add 14 g (½ oz) Chinook hops for last 40 minutes.
- Add Irish moss for last 30 minutes.
- Add Hallertau hops for last 20 minutes.
- Add Northern Brewer at end of boil.
- Cool wort quickly and pitch yeast.
- Primary-ferment for 7–10 days at 18.3–21.1°C (65–70°F).
- Rack to secondary and ferment for 14 days at 7.2–10°C (45–50°F).
- Bottle, using corn sugar.
- Age in bottle for 7–10 days.

Fruit beers

Raspberry Amber

Peter A'Hearn
Home Brew Mart

Peter's verdict: "The fruit purée is aseptic so you don't have to worry about contamination. For a more intriguing brew, try using White Labs Trappist ale yeast."

454 g (1 lb) crystal malt (60 L)
3.1 kg (7 lb) pale malt extract
28.3 g (1 oz) Progress hops (5·7% alpha)
28.3 g (1 oz) Progress hops
White Labs British ale yeast
1 can Oregon brand raspberry purée
47.2 g (½ cup) corn sugar (priming)

METHOD

- Add grains to water and heat to boil. Remove grains.
- Remove from heat and stir in extract. Return to boil.
- When wort is boiling, add 28.3 g (1 oz) Progress hops (60 minutes in boil).
- Add 28.3 g (1 oz) Progress hops during last five minutes of boil.
- Cool wort quickly and pitch yeast.
- Primary-ferment for 7–10 days.
- Rack to secondary and add purée.
- Leave in secondary for 7 days.
- Bottle with 47.2 g (½ cup) corn sugar.

Assessing Your Brew

Listen for the healthy sound of escaping CO_2 as you open the bottle. Watch as the bubbles rush to the surface. Note the clarity and color of the brew. Smell the array of aromas, and learn to discern the many flavors of beer. Most of all, enjoy the beer that you have created!

The American Homebrewers Association hosts and sponsors many competitions every year. Entering your beer into a competition will give you an objective assessment of the quality of your homebrew, and the certified judges will offer ways to improve your beer.

You can use the same criteria at home to evaluate your beer. A simple test, as suggested by homebrew experts such as Charlie Papazian, Dave Miller, Gregg Smith, and Fred Ekhardt, utilizes a 20-point system, broken down as follows:

4 Overall impression 1–3 points
- *Does the beer represent its style?*
- *Is it drinkable?*
- *Are there any odd or off flavors?*

1 Bouquet and aroma 0–4 points
- *Hop bouquet*
- *Aroma from malt, other fermentables*

2 Appearance 0–3 points
- *Clarity*
- *Color*
- *Head retention*

3 Taste 10 points
- *Balance between malt and hops*
- *Mouth-feel (light–heavy)*
- *Aftertaste*

The easiest way to learn recipe formulation is to find a homebrew recipe and, to use a musical analogy, "riff" off that. The two major factors involved in how your beer will turn out are technique and ingredients. Hone the first by brewing a single recipe until you achieve consistent results. Then, substitute one ingredient at a time, keeping detailed notes on how the beer looks, tastes, etc. For example, if you are brewing Hoppy Gurkha's IPA, try a darker- or lighter-colored crystal malt. Substitute dry extract for syrup (making the appropriate quantity adjustment). Change the yeast strain to a liquid American style, or change the variety of hops. Make only one change per batch and record differences in outcome.

Your technique will also alter your homebrew. By replacing a percentage of extract with a compatible grain, your brew will turn out different. Partial-mash brewers have the advantage of freshness and control, though considerations such as extract yield must be taken into account. Preparing a yeast starter may result in a more highly attenuated brew. The addition of a wort chiller to your system can aid in clarity and flavor. Altering hopping schedules will affect the bitterness and flavor, as will the form of hops that you are using. Specific gravity, color, and bitterness are the three factors to consider when devising your own recipe or experimenting with published recipes. If you are brewing a specific style, you'll want to stay within the parameters of that style. Let's take a look at gravity, bitterness, and color, and see how each is affected by varying ingredients and techniques.

Gravity

THE SPECIFIC GRAVITY of a wort is the measurement of all the fermentable sugars and unfermentable dextrins swimming around in your fermenter at a given time. Original gravity is the amount before fermentation, and final gravity is the amount remaining after the yeast have metabolized much of the matter. All malts and adjuncts add varying amounts of gravity, or density, to your wort. They don't, however, all proffer the same amount of sugars and dextrins, nor do they all contribute identical flavor. The variety of malt (six-row or two-row), the degree of modification, and the amount of time spent in the kiln all determine the flavor, color, and gravity given by a specific malt. Likewise, adjuncts and other fermentable additions each have their own unique characteristics.

There are, however, a few basic malts that generally make up the bulk of fermentable compounds in all styles of beer. A loose but somewhat fitting analogy is to compare these grains to a pizza crust. There are only a few types of crust. Yet everyone has a favorite type of pizza. Some like pepperoni, some mushroom, some sausage. There is a huge variety of pizza available, but each must have some basic crust underneath to support the sauces, cheese, and toppings. If adjuncts and specialty grains help distinguish different styles of beer, then basic brewer's malt is the crust that makes it all possible. Lager and Pilsner malts are the basis for lagers: the former for pale and dark lagers, as well as some ales, and the latter for Pilsners and other light lagers. Pale-ale malt constitutes a large portion of the grain bill in most British ales, from pale to porter. The sweeter and somewhat deeper-colored Vienna malt is often used as the basis for Oktoberfest and Marzen lagers. The amber, aromatic Munich malt is used in some German lagers, and as a flavoring malt in many other beers. Wheat malt often contributes up to 50 percent of the grain bill for weizens, wits, and other wheat beers.

When you purchase an extract, you are often getting a combination of one of the above malts with some percentage of specialty malt. While a light malt extract may be mainly composed of mashed pale malt, dark malt extract may be a blend of pale malt with darker specialty malts, such as chocolate or roasted malt. Hence the all-extract brewer can produce a dark stout without the addition of specialty grains. However, it is important to note that even the darkest extract is prepared with mostly two-row pale-ale malt, and then colored with dark crystal, black patent, or chocolate malt. None of these last three can constitute a large part of the extract, because none contains the starch-converting enzymes needed in a proper mash.

When I partial-mash, I like to use lighter extracts and add malts to attain body, color, and flavor. For example, I may substitute a portion of extract for pale-ale malt when making a stout. Then I can add a pound or so of dark specialty malt to achieve proper color. Consult the Malt Profiles table at the back of the book for a brief description of various malts.

Swapping malts

You can easily use dry malt extract in a recipe calling for extract syrup, and vice versa. Since syrup contains up to 20 percent water, it supplies less gravity per pound than does DME. If a recipe calls for DME, multiply the amount by 1·2 to determine how much syrup to use. Conversely, if a recipe calls for extract syrup, multiply the amount by 0·8 to find out how much DME to add.

You can also replace a portion of extract with grain. However, simply replacing a pound of extract with a pound of pale-ale malt will result in a lower original gravity. Whenever you mash and sparge, you inevitably leave some fermentables behind. If you want to substitute malt for a portion of your extract, or convert an all-grain recipe to extract, use the following formulas:

To convert extract to grain:

lb malt extract syrup x 1·23 = lb pale malt
lb dry malt extract x 1·45 = lb pale malt
lb wheat malt extract x 1·07 = lb wheat malt

To find out how much extract to use in place of malt, use the following:

lb pale malt x 0·8125 = lb malt extract syrup
lb pale malt x 0·6875 = lb dry malt extract
lb wheat malt x 0·937 = lb wheat malt extract

Say you have a recipe that calls for 6·6 pounds liquid malt extract, and you want to substitute a pound of pale malt. How much extract would you need to add to achieve the same original gravity? First, convert the one pound of malt to extract using the formula:

lb pale malt x 0·8125 = lb malt extract syrup

So, one pound of pale malt × 0·8125 = 0·8125 pounds malt extract syrup. Next, subtract the product from the total extract, to find the extract needed to get the same OG:

6·6 – 0·8125 = 5·36 lb malt extract syrup

For the record, it's a lot easier to weigh dry malt extract than it is to weigh extract syrup.

Bitterness

WHILE THE DEGREE of bitterness may vary from style to style, all beer is balanced with hops. Bitterness is the result of isomerized alpha acids, which dissolve into solution during the boil. To calculate bitterness, measured as IBUs, use the Hop Utilization table found in the back of the book. By looking up IBUs in the Beer Style Guidelines table, you can devise a hopping schedule that matches the parameters of your chosen style.

When devising recipes, some brewers go over the top with hops. So-called "hop heads," dizzy with a love of the bittering flower, add lupulin with a lupine appetite. However, too much of a good thing can cause a harsh bite that borders on astringency. Stay cool, beware the moon, and don't overdo it with the hops.

Higher-gravity beers tolerate heavy hop additions better than lighter brews. The reason is simple. Higher gravities means more sugars, which means more sweetness to absorb the bitterness of the hop. A barley wine or imperial stout is highly hopped to counterbalance the huge malt additions.

Flavor and bouquet

While all hops contain essential oils, certain varieties are especially suited and, therefore, cultivated to supply distinctive hop aromas and flavors. Cascade, Kent Goldings, and Saaz hops come to mind. Each variety is prized for its aromatic properties, yet each has a unique flavor that testifies to the range and complexity found within the lupulin glands of the hop plant. The use of Kent Goldings hops distinguishes British pale ales from all others. The classic, mild aroma and flavor are in stark contrast to those of the floral, citrusy Cascade hop–a popular finishing hop in American pale ales. No one can deny the demarcative signature that the Saaz hop gives to Bohemian Pilsners. The spicy aroma and flavor make it truly unique.

When choosing a finishing hop, decide what quality or qualities you want to achieve. Volatile oils are lost quickly, so purchase only the freshest hops that are sealed in nitrogen-purged bags and stored under refrigeration. Confine your additions to late in the boil, add them directly after the boil, or dry-hop in a secondary fermenter.

Most of all, experiment with different varieties of hops until you perceive how each affects the aroma and flavor of your home-brew. All of the descriptive adjectives and similes in the world fail to convey what your senses will tell you through experience.

Color

Color is determined by the type of malt used, the length and intensity of the boil, the rate of cooling to pitching temperatures, the strain of yeast used, and a number of other factors. In the intermediate section, I showed you a simple and popular method for predicting final color, based on the Lovibond rating assigned to each malt. This formula will give you a rough estimate of how light or dark your beer will be, based on Homebrew Color Units. This scale, however, doesn't correspond very well with the SRM color scale. Still, in the absence of expensive equipment or access to a lab, HCUs offer some approximation.

Color is, perhaps, the most difficult quality to predict and quantify. Using the Malt Profiles table in the back of the book, along with the simple HCU formula, will give you a starting point. Experience will serve to sharpen your intuition. Homebrewing is a blend of science and art. When science is beyond your means, you need to hone your artistic sensibilities.

CHAPTER NINE

For Your Reference

Tables

CALCULATIONS TABLES

The following tables will help you understand how ingredients contribute to the final characteristics of your homebrew, and are a starting point for concocting your own recipes. While these formulas appear in earlier chapters, they are compiled here for easy reference when filling out your Homebrew Worksheets.

DETERMINING SPECIFIC GRAVITY

Using tables three and four, you can gain a rough estimate of the original gravity that various malts, adjuncts, and sugars will give to your wort. As a general rule, you can assume that the final gravity will be approximately one fourth that of the original gravity.

$$\frac{\text{SG of fermentable x lbs added} + \text{SG of fermentable x lbs added}}{\text{Volume of beer brewed}} = \text{OG}$$

SWAPPING MALTS

Extract to Extract

1 lb malt extract syrup = 0·8 lb dry malt extract

1 lb dry malt extract = 1·2 lb malt extract syrup

Extract to Grain

lbs malt extract syrup × 1·23 = lbs pale malt

lbs dry malt extract × 1·45 = lbs pale malt

lbs wheat malt extract × 1·07 = lbs wheat malt

Grain to Extract

lbs pale malt × 0·8125 = lbs malt extract syrup

lbs pale malt × 0·6875 = lbs dry malt extract

lbs wheat malt × 0·937 = lbs wheat malt extract

DETERMINING APPARENT ATTENUATION PERCENTAGE

AAP = [(original gravity – final gravity) / original gravity] × 100

PREDICTING COLOR

Tables three and four also contain SRM information that can be used to approximate the color that each addition will supply to your brew. Your results will be expressed as HCUs (Homebrew Color Units). The equation is just like the one for determining original gravity. When you buy malt the color may be designated by degrees Lovibond. Consider these the same as SRM.

$$\frac{\text{SG of fermentable x lbs added} + \text{SG of fermentable x lbs added}}{\text{Volume of beer brewed}} = \text{HCUs}$$

Homebrew Color Units do not correspond with SRMs. A rough description of HCUs is as follows:

HCU	COLOR
1–5	Light yellow to dark yellow
6–10	Golden to light amber
11–20	Amber to dark amber
21–30	Dark amber to copper
31–40	Copper
41–50	Copper to brown
51–80	Brown to black
85–	Black

Note: Data derived from *Designing Great Beers*, by Ray Daniels; *Homebrewing Guide*, by Dave Miller; and *The Brewer's Companion*, by Randy Mosher.

PREDICTING BITTERNESS

Use Glenn Tinseth's Hop Utilization Table to find alpha acid utilization rates based on wort gravity and time hops spend in the boil.

IBUs = decimal alpha acid utilization × mg/l of added alpha acids

To calculate mg/l of added alpha acids, use:

$$\text{Mg/l of added alpha acids} = \frac{\text{Decimal AA rating x oz hops x 7490}}{\text{Volume of finished beer in gallons}}$$

TABLE 2
BEER STYLE GUIDELINES

KEY: OG = Original Gravity   FG = Final Gravity   IBUs = International Bittering Units
SRM = Standard Reference Measurement

BEER STYLE	OG	FG	IBUs	SRM
ALES				
Belgian Strong Ale	1·062 –1·095	1·011 –1·023	20–50	3–7 (light)
				7–20 (dark)
Flanders Brown	1·040 –1·055	1·006 –1·015	10–25	10–20
Lambic	1·045 –1·056	1·000 –1·010	11–23	6–14
Belgian Pale Ale	1·044 –1·096	1·008 –1·024	25–45	4–12
Trappist	1·044 –1·096	1·008 –1·024	25–45	4–12
Dubbel	1·050 –1·070	1·012 –1·016	18–30	10–18
Trippel	1·065 –1·096	1·018 –1·024	18–30	4–7
Wit	1·044 –1·050	1·006 –1·010	18–28	2–4
Barley Wine	1·085 –1·120	1·024 –1·032	50–100	14–30
Bitter	1·035 –1·050	1·006 –1·014	25–55	8–12
English IPA	1·050 –1·068	1·012 –1·018	40–60	6–18
English Pale Ale	1·044 –1·056	1·008 –1·016	20–40	4–11
Porter	1·045 –1·060	1·008 –1·016	25–40	30+
Scottish Ales	1·035 –1·050	1·010 –1·018	10–25	10–25
Scotch Ale	1·072 –1·085	1·016 –1·028	25–35	10–30
Stout (Dry)	1·038 –1·045	1·008 –1·014	30–40	40+
Stout (Sweet)	1·045 –1·056	1·012 –1·020	15–25	40+
Imperial Stout	1·075 –1·095	1·020 –1·032	50–85	20+
Strong Ale/English Old Ale	1·055 –1·125	1·010 –1·040	25–75	15–20
Bière De Garde	1·060 –1·075	1·012 –1·014	25–30	8–12
Alt	1·042 –1·050	1·006 –1·014	28–45	11–19
Dunkelweizen	1·046 –1·056	1·008 –1·016	10–15	11–18
Hefe-weizen	1·046 –1·056	1·008 –1·016	10–15	3–9
Weizen	1·046 –1·056	1·008 –1·016	10–15	3–9
Weizenbock	1·066 –1·080	1·016 –1·028	10–15	7–30
American Pale Ale	1·044 –1·056	1·008 –1·016	20–40	4–10
American IPA	1·052 –1·070	1·012 –1·018	40–65	8–14
LAGERS				
Vienna	1·048 –1·056	1·012 –1·018	22–28	8–12
Bohemian Pilsner	1·044 –1·056	1·014 –1·020	30–45	3–5
Bock	1·066 –1·074	1·018 –1·024	20–30	18–28
Doppelbock	1·074 –1·082	1·020 –1·030	17–27	12–30
Helles Bock	1·066 –1·068	1·012 –1·020	20–35	4–8
Dortmunder	1·048 –1·056	1·010 –1·014	20–38	3–6
Munich Dunkel	1·050 –1·056	1·012 –1·018	18–27	14–20
Munich Helles	1·044 –1·052	1·008 –1·012	20–30	4–6
German Pilsner	1·048 –1·050	1·006 –1·012	30–40	3–4
Rauchbier	1·048 –1·052	1·012 –1·016	20–30	10–20
Schwarzbier	1·044 –1·052	1·012 –1·016	20–30	25–30
California Common	1·042 –1·055	1·012 –1·018	35–45	8–17

TABLE 3
MALT PROFILES

Potential extract for 1 lb malt in 1 gallon of water at 60°F

The following malts can be used to 100% in all grain brewing
and must be mashed

MALT & COUNTRY	SG	SRM	DESCRIPTION
2-row Pale Malt US	1·037	2–4	Well modified with a high diastastic power. Can be substituted for light malt extract in partial mashing. Often used for ales and lagers.
6-row Pale Malt US	1·035	1–2	High enzyme content makes it a good partner in a high-adjunct mash. Considered inferior to 2-row variety in flavor and clarity.
Lager Malt (Klages) US	1·036	1–2	Can be substituted for a portion of extract in the production of lagers.
Pilsner Malt Europe	1·036	1–2	Low enzyme content and large husk to starch ratio prohibits partial-mash additions beyond 20% of total grain bill. Used often in Pilsners and bocks.
Pale Ale Malt 2-row Belgium, Britain	1·037	1–2	Relatively low in enzymes, this malt can, nonetheless, convert well using a single-infusion mash. Used in the production of all British ales.
Vienna Malt Europe, US, Canada	1·036	4–5	Amber and sweet, this malt is used in Vienna, Marzen, and Oktoberfest lagers.
Mild Ale Malt Britain	1·036	3–6	This is pale ale malt that has been further kilned to deepen husk color. Mild malt imparts a sweet nutty flavor to dark British ales, like milds and browns.
Munich Malt Europe, US, Canada	1·036	5–10	Similar to the mild ale, this malt gives beers a deep orange-reddish color and imparts a rich aroma and toasted grain taste.
Wheat Malt Europe, US	1·038	1–3	Can be used in small quantities for partial-mash brewing. Used in the production of wheat beers, and in small amounts to aid in head retention. For single-infusion mashing, use wheat malt extract for the bulk of your grist.

The following specialty malts and grains contribute various characteristics to your beer, but do not need to be mashed.

GRAIN & COUNTRY	SG	SRM	DESCRIPTION
CaraPils/Dextrine Malt	1·033	1–2	Used to enhance body in lighter beers without imparting appreciable color. Slow kilning keeps this crystal malt light.
Victory Malt	1·036	3–5	Used in dark ales and lagers to add a toasty flavor.
Light Crystal Malt	1·033	10–25	Both light and dark crystal malts add sweetness, body from dextrins, and color to a variety of ales. These specialty malts are popular in pale ales and IPAs. Check the packaging for specific Lovibond ratings.
Dark Crystal Malt	1·031	60–150	See above.
Biscuit Malt	1·035	23–50	Used in brown ales and other dark beers. Imparts a warm, toasty, biscuit-like flavor.
Chocolate Malt	1·032	325–450	Pale malt is roasted until a chocolate color is reached. Lends a roasted flavor to dark ales, like porter and stout.
Black Patent Malt	1·030	500–700	Also used in porters and stouts, this malt is kilned longer than chocolate malt, resulting in the charcoal-black color. Used in small amounts for coloring and lending a burnt, sometimes bitter flavor.
Roasted Barley	1·035	400–500	Similar to black patent, but this unmalted barley is drier in flavor and aroma. Can impart coffee-like flavors to dry stouts, and is used to deepen the color of mild and Scottish ales.

The following is a list of both dry and syrup malt extracts. Since no two extract brands are composed of the same ingredients, it is impossible to pinpoint the qualities they will give to your homebrew. Ask your local supply dealer for information on specific brands. Also, consult the manufacturer and other homebrewers to find which brand delivers the best and most consistent results. While some people find it easier to work with syrup (it doesn't clump in the wort), DME has a longer shelf life and is more potent. Finally, make sure your extract is marked "unhopped" before you buy it. This gives you more control over the destiny of your homebrew!

EXTRACT	SG	SRM	DESCRIPTION
Light Syrup	1·040	3–6	While many extracts purport to be made entirely of malted barley, some are adulterated with such additives as glucose and caramel coloring. Experiment with different brands until you find the few that deliver consistent results.
Amber Syrup	1·040	10–18	See above
Dark Syrup	1·040	35–65	See above
Pale DME	1·047	4–8	See above
Amber DME	1·047	10–35	See above
Dark DME	1·047	45–100	See above

TABLE 4
ADJUNCT AND SUGAR PROFILES

Adjuncts are unmalted grains, which can be used, in small quantities, to influence the character of your homebrew in many ways.

ADJUNCT	SG	SRM	DESCRIPTION
Flaked Barley	1·028–1·034	1–3	Small additions add flavor and body to dark beers. Mash along with other grains.
Flaked Corn	1·035–1·039	0	Often used in large amounts by breweries that wish to add potency and cut costs. Small amounts may add character to lighter beer, but flaked corn must be partial-mashed with an enzyme-rich pale malt.
Flaked Oats	1·030–1·035	2–3	Used in oatmeal stout and Belgian witbier. Small amounts impart a smooth mouth-feel, enhance body, add a grainy flavor, and aid in head retention.
Flaked Rice	1·037–1·039	0	Adds potency to light beers, but imparts little else.
Flaked Rye	1·032–1·036	1–3	Rye imparts a dry flavor to beer that is distinct and pronounced. Some people love the taste, but it's not for everyone.
Flaked Wheat	1·030–1·036	1–2	Can be used in Belgian wheat beers for added acidity. Small amounts also aid in head retention. Partial-mash with a well-modified malt.

Sugars can be used to condition beer, lighten body and flavor, or add character to certain styles of beer.

SUGAR	DESCRIPTION
Cane sugar	Used to boost potency and lighten color. Not recommended.
Corn sugar	Essentially glucose. Used mainly as a priming agent for conditioning.
Candi sugar	Used in many strong Belgian beers to lighten body.
Invert sugar	Used in many Belgian beers to boost potency.
Honey	Used to lighten color and body. Also used to make mead.
Treacle	Sometimes used to flavor stouts.
Turbinado	Small amounts used in some pale ales and strong ales.
Molasses	Similar to treacle, sometimes used in darker beers.
Milk sugar	Derived from milk, milk sugar is lactose, an unfermentable sugar used to sweeten stouts.

TABLE 5
HOP PROFILES

The following hops are primarily used as bittering hops. These should be boiled for a minimum of 20 minutes to extract the alpha resins.

VARIETY	ORIGIN	AA%	STORABILITY	DESCRIPTION
Admiral	Britain	11–14	Fair	Similar to Target, but higher in alpha acids.
Brewers Gold	Germany, US	7–10	Poor	Popular bittering hop can be used in many ale recipes. Especially suited for dark, heavy ales and lagers.
Chinook	US	11–14	Good	Very bitter and pungent. Used primarily for porters and stouts.
Cluster	US	5·5–9	Very Good	Very popular in the US, this mild bittering hop has a unique aroma that some people like.
Eroica	US	10–13	Fair	Very bitter hop, used in many beers of medium to high gravity.
Galena	US	10–14	Very Good	Versatile and potent, this hop is popular with British and American brewers.
Green Bullet	New Zealand	10–11	Good	Used primarily in Australian lagers. Very bitter!
Northern Brewer	Germany, Britain	7–10	Good	Used in California common beers, German lagers, and British ales. Northern brewer is pungent, assertive and bitter.
Nugget	US	10–14	Good	A little goes a long way. This super-alpha hop is very bitter and aromatic. Used in many styles of beer.
Pride of Ringwood	Australia	7–10	Fair	Popular bittering hop in Australia, this hybrid bittering hop is growing in popularity.
Target	Britain	10–13	Poor	Widely used in Britain as a bittering hop.
Zenith	Britain	8–10	Good	Relatively new hop, developed in Britain. Bitter, with some aroma.

Dual hops can be used as bittering agents, and contain the essential oils needed to provide flavor and aroma. These can be introduced throughout boil.

VARIETY	ORIGIN	AA%	STORAGE	DESCRIPTION
Bullion	Britain, US	6–10	Poor	Bitter, but with pungent, spicy aroma and flavor.
Centennial	US	9–11	Fair	Strong bittering hop with Cascade-like aroma and flavor.
Challenger	Britain	7–9.5	Poor	Used in British and Belgian ales for bittering. However, home-brewers are discovering its aromatic qualities. Rare in the US.
Columbus	US	12–15.5	Fair	The high end of dual hops. Great for bittering and aroma. Used in American pale ales, stouts, and porters.
Hallertauer	Germany	3.5–6.5	Poor	Clean bittering hop with a soft, spicy flavor. Popular and versatile.
Northdown	Britain	7.5–10	Good	Good bittering, flavor, and aroma hop.
Perle	Germany, US	6–9.5	Good	Similar to Hallertauer, this is used as both a bittering and aromatic hop. Used in German lagers, and Canadian lagers.
Spalter	Germany, US	3.5–5	Fair	Very refined hop flavor and aroma. Popular as a replacement to super-alpha bittering hops, because of its clean finish. Just use more.
Spalter Select	Germany	4–6	Good	Newer, heartier form of Spalter. Used for bittering and aroma.
Sryrian Goldings	Slovenia	5–7	Fair	Fairly neutral finish, a good aromatic for styles that require a soft bouquet. Popular in lagers, Marzen, and some Belgian ales.
Tettnanger	Germany, US	3–5.5	Poor	Floral, spicy aroma, used in wheat ales and many lagers.

Finishing hops are generally low in alpha acids and high in essential oils. Since the oils dissipate quickly, they should be introduced late into the boil, steeped after the boil, or dry hopped.

VARIETY	ORIGIN	AA%	STORAGE	DESCRIPTION
Cascade	US	4–7	Poor	Immensely popular aroma hops in the US. Widely used in American pale ales and IPAs. Floral, citrusy aroma and flavor.
Crystal	US	2–5	Poor	Recently developed, resembles Halletauer.
Fuggles	Britain, US	4–6	Poor	Distinctive British flavor. Crowns British pales, porters, and stouts.
Golding	US, Canada Britain	3–5	Fair	Classic British hop with a distinctive flavor and aroma. Used in lighter ales.
Kent Golding	Britain	4–6	Poor	Quintessential English flavoring hop. Refined spicy bouquet and aroma. Used in many quality British beers.
Liberty	US	3.5–5	Poor	New variety, similar to Halletauer, but spicier. Used in German lagers and American ales.
Mt Hood	US	3–5.5	Poor	Another fine outgrowth of the legendary Halletauer hop.
Saaz	Czech Repulic	3.5–6	Poor	Famous Czech hop used in classic Pilsners for its fine, spicy aroma and flavor. Also used in Belgian wheat ales.
Strissel Spalt	France	3–5	Fair	Used in many continental beers, famous in the rural Bière De Garde.
Ultra	US	2–3.5	Fair	New, disease-resistant hop, similar to Saaz.
Willamette	US	4–6	Fair	An American northwestern finishing hop, similar to, but more potent than, the English Fuggles. A very high-quality and popular hop. Used in a variety of British and American ales.

TABLE 6
GLENN TINSETH'S HOP UTILIZATION TABLE
Decimal alpha acid utilization vs. boil time and wort original gravity

BOIL TIME	ORIGINAL GRAVITY								
(minutes)	1·030	1·040	1·050	1·060	1·070	1·080	1·090	1·100	1·110
0	0·000	0·000	0·000	0·000	0·000	0·000	0·000	0·000	0·000
3	0·034	0·031	0·029	0·026	0·024	0·022	0·020	0·018	0·017
6	0·065	0·059	0·054	0·049	0·045	0·041	0·038	0·035	0·032
9	0·092	0·084	0·077	0·070	0·064	0·059	0·054	0·049	0·045
12	0·116	0·106	0·097	0·088	0·081	0·074	0·068	0·062	0·056
15	0·137	0·125	0·114	0·105	0·096	0·087	0·080	0·073	0·067
18	0·156	0·142	0·130	0·119	0·109	0·099	0·091	0·083	0,076
21	0·173	0·158	0·144	0·132	0·120	0·110	0·101	0·092	0·084
24	0·187	0·171	0·157	0·143	0·131	0·120	0·109	0·100	0·191
27	0·201	0·183	0·168	0·153	0·140	0·128	0·117	0·107	0·098
30	0·212	0·194	0·177	0·162	0·148	0·135	0·124	0·113	0·103
33	0·223	0·203	0·186	0·170	0·155	0·142	0·130	0·119	0·108
36	0·232	0·212	0·194	0·177	0·162	0·148	0·135	0·124	0·113
39	0·240	0·219	0·200	0·183	0·167	0·153	0·140	0·128	0·117
42	0·247	0·226	0·206	0·189	0·172	0·158	0·144	0·132	0·120
45	0·253	0·232	0·212	0·194	0·177	0·162	0·148	0·135	0·123
48	0·259	0·237	0·216	0·198	0·181	0·165	0·151	0·138	0·126
51	0·264	0·241	0·221	0·202	0·184	0·169	0·154	0·141	0·129
54	0·269	0·246	0·224	0·205	0·188	0·171	0·157	0·143	0·131
57	0·273	0·249	0·228	0·208	0·190	0·174	0·159	0·145	0·133
60	0·276	0·252	0·231	0·211	0·193	0·176	0·161	0·147	0·135
70	0·285	0·261	0·238	0·218	0·199	0·182	0·166	0·152	0·139
80	0·291	0·266	0·243	0·222	0·203	0·186	0·170	0·155	0·142
90	0·295	0·270	0·247	0·226	0·206	0·188	0·172	0·157	0·144
120	0·301	0·275	0·252	0·230	0·210	0·192	0·176	0·161	0·147

EXTRACT HOMEBREW WORKSHEET

Name of Beer	Style	Date Brewed	Time of Boil

HOMEBREW RECIPE

EQUIPMENT/INGREDIENT CHECKLIST & PROCEDURAL SCHEDULE

EQUIPMENT	INGREDIENTS	TIME(S) ADDED	
	NOTES	**NOTES**	

POST-BOIL PROCEDURES & RESULTS

FERMENTATION	BOTTLING	RESULTS
OG:	Date Bottled:	
Pitching Temp:	Date of 1st tasting:	
Cooling Time:	Date of 2nd tasting:	
Started fermenting:		
Racked? y/n Days:		
Ceased fermenting:		
FG:		

INTERMEDIATE HOMEBREW RECIPE/WORKSHEET

Name of Beer   Style   Date Brewed   Time of Boil

HOMEBREW RECIPE

INGREDIENT CHARACTERISTICS BREAKDOWN

Key: G = Gravity °L = Lovibond α% = AA% TIME = Time Spent in Boil% U% = (decimal) Utilization ATTN% = Attenuation

MALT/ADJ	LBS	G	°L	HOPS	OZ	α%	TIME	U%	M/C	YEAST	ATTN%

TARGET HOMEBREW CHARACTERISTICS

OG: **FG:**   **HCU:**   **IBU:**   **Other:**

EQUIPMENT/PROCEDURAL NOTES

Heat Source: Cooling Method:

HOMEBREW FLOWCHART: HOT SIDE

PRE-BOIL

I Grains	II Malt Extracts	III Adjuncts	IV Brew Salts	
1) Time Added:	1) Time Added:	1) Time Added:	1) Time Added:	
Temp Added:		2) Time Added:	Amount Added:	
2) Time Removed:			2) Time Added:	
Temp Removed:			Amount Added:	
NOTES	**NOTES**	**NOTES**	**NOTES**	

BOIL

V Boiling Hops		VI Clarifiers		VII Finishing hops	
1) Time(s)	Amount(s)	1) Time(s)	Amount(s)	1) Time(s)	Amount(s)
NOTES		**NOTES**		**NOTES**	

HOMEBREW FLOWCHART: COLD SIDE

COOLING/PITCHING

VIII Cooling	IX Pitching Yeast:	
1) Time wort removed from heat:	1) Temp yeast pitched:	
2) Took how long to cool?:	2) Amount pitched:	
NOTES	**NOTES**	

FERMENTING/CONDITIONING

X Primary Fermentation	XI Aging
1) Vessel:	1) Date racked:
2) Ambient temp:	
3) Date/Time started fermenting:	3) Dry hops: Form: Amount:
4) Date fermentation ceased:	4) Ambient temp:
NOTES	**NOTES**

PRIMING/BOTTLING

XII Priming/Bottling				
1) Priming agent:	Amount:	2) Bottled	Kegged	Other
3) Ambient storage temp:		Stored how long?		
NOTES				

HOMEBREW RESULTS/JOURNAL

RESULTS

Predicted OG:	Actual OG:	Predicted FG:	Actual FG:	Alcohol %:
Calculated IBUs:	Perceived bitterness:			
Calculated HCU:	Resultant color:			
Desired aroma/flavor From hops:		Perceived aroma/flavor:		
Desired malt flavors:		Perceived malt flavors:		
Desired body:		Resultant body:		
Off/odd flavors:				
Overall impression:				
NOTES/IMPRESSIONS/FUTURE GOALS				

Glossary

Adjunct: any unmalted grain used in brewing.

Ale: a class of beer fermented at warm temperatures using a top-fermenting strain of yeast.

Alpha acids: soluble hop resin that provides bitterness to beer. Alpha acids are measured as a percentage of the total weight of the hop flower.

Alpha acid units (AAU): a formula used by homebrewers to determine the amount of alpha acids derived from boiling hops. AAU = alpha acid percentage multiplied by the amount of hops used, in ounces.

Alpha amylase: a diastastic enzyme in barley that breaks down starches into dextrin chains. *See beta amylase.*

Attenuation: the degree to which yeast converts sugars in wort into ethyl alcohol and carbon dioxide.

Autolysis: a process in which yeast cells digest each other after most of the sugars in the wort are metabolized. Causes an unpleasant flavor and aroma. This can be avoided if fermented beer is promptly racked off the yeast sediment.

Barley: a cereal grain which has been a main ingredient in beer for nearly ten thousand years.

Beers: a fermented beverage made from malt, hops, yeast, and water.

Beta acids: harsh, bitter hop resins which are normally insoluble.

Beta amylase: a diastastic enzyme in barley that breaks down dextrins into shorter glucose chains. *See alpha amylase.*

Brewing liquor: term for water used in brewing.

Chill haze: cloudiness in beer that occurs when residual proteins and tannins coagulate in suspension with a temperature decrease. This can result from improper mashing temperatures, oversparging, and irregularities in the fermentation process.

Cold break: the precipitation of proteins that occurs when wort is quickly chilled.

Conditioning: the process of adding carbon dioxide to beer by allowing yeast to metabolize a small amount of sugar in a sealed keg or bottle.

Dextrins: unfermentable carbohydrate chains which add body to beer.

Diacetyl: a compound formed during fermentation that imparts a taste and aroma of butter or butterscotch.

Diastastic power: a measure of the amount of alpha and beta amylase in a quantity of malt.

Dry hopping: the addition of hops to a secondary fermenter.

Esters: a class of compounds formed during fermentation, which impart fruity flavors and aromas to beer.

Ethyl alcohol: the intoxicating agent in beer.

Fermentation: the process by which yeast metabolize wort sugars and excrete ethyl alcohol and carbon dioxide through anaerobic respiration.

Grist: crushed malt and adjuncts which are mixed with hot water to form a mash.

Homebrew color units (HCU): a formula used to predict the color of homebrew based on malt color. Color of malt (Lovibond) x amount used (lbs) ÷ volume of finished beer (gallons).

Hops: a member of the vine-growing family, *Humulus lupulus*, which is used in brewing to provide bitterness and aroma.

Hot break: the precipitation of proteins that occurs when the wort is initially brought to a boil.

Hydrometer: an instrument that measures specific gravity, degrees Plato, and alcohol by volume in wort and beer.

International bittering units (IBU): the measure of bitterness in beer based on parts per million of dissolved iso-alpha acids in a liter of beer.

Isomerization: a rearrangement of atoms in a compound. In brewing, the rearrangement of alpha acids into soluble isomers brought on by boiling.

Krausen: the thick, foamy head that forms during the early stages of fermentation.

Lager: a class of beer fermented at cool temperatures using a bottom-fermenting strain of yeast. Also, the process of storing fermenting beer at cold temperatures to produce lager.

Lautering: the process of separating sweet wort from the spent grains after mashing is complete.

Lees: yeast sediment that is removed from fermented wort for use in future batches of beer.

Lovibond: an old (but widely used) color scale for malt.

Malt: any grain that has been modified for use in brewing.

Mash: the mixture of hot water and grist. Also, the act of converting malt starches into sugars by exposing the crushed grains to hot water.

Mineral salts: dissolved compounds in water that aid in the brewing process.

Modification: the changes in a grain that occur during germination.

Nose: term used to describe the aroma of beer.

Oxidation: the negative reaction between oxygen and various components in wort and beer that results in stale or "wet cardboard"-like flavors.

Oxygenation: the process of adding oxygen to cool wort to aid in the growth cycle of yeast.

Palate: term used to describe the general flavor of beer.

Priming: the act of adding sugar before bottling or kegging to produce carbonation.

Racking: transferring wort or beer from one vessel to another.

Reinheitsgebot: the German purity law of 1516 which allows only malt, hops, water, and yeast to be used in brewing.

Sanitation: the use of certain chemicals to remove microorganisms from clean brewing equipment.

Secondary fermenter: a sealed vessel used to mature beer after primary fermentation.

Slurry: a mushy soup formed by adding dry yeast to warm water.

Sparging: the act of rinsing surplus sugars from spent grains by sprinkling hot water over the grain bed.
Specific gravity: the measure of wort density at a given time. Original gravity is the density of wort prior to pitching. Final gravity is the density of beer after fermentation.
Standard reference method (SRM): a system used to measure the color of beer.

Tannins: compounds derived from a grain husk that can cause haze and astringency in the finished beer.
Trub: the protein sediment in wort that forms after the hot and cold breaks.
Wort: the sweet, dense mixture of dextrins, sugars, and hops material prior to fermentation.
Yeast: a single-celled fungus that changes wort into beer through fermentation.

Bibliography

Books

Burch, Byron. *Brewing Quality Beers: The Home Brewer's Essential Guidebook*, second edition. Fulton, CA: Joby Books, 1994.

Daniels, Ray. *Designing Great Beers: The Ultimate Guide to Brewing Classic Beer Styles*. Boulder, CO: Brewers Publications, 1996.

Fix, George. *Principles of Brewing Science*. Boulder, CO: Brewers Publications, 1989.

Garetz, Mark. *Using Hops: The Complete Guide to Hops for the Craft Brewer*. Danville, CA: HopTech, 1994.

Jackson, Michael. *Michael Jackson's Beer Companion*, second edition. Philadelphia, PA: Running Press, 1997.

Janson, Lee. *Brew Chem 101*. Pownal, VT: Story Publishing, 1996.

Line, Dave. *The Big Book of Brewing*. Andover, U.K: Amateur Winemaker Publications Ltd, 1979.

Lutzen Karl F. and Mark Stevens. *Brew Ware: How to Find, Adapt & Build Homebrewing Equipment*. Pownal, VT: Story Publishing, 1996.

Mares, William. *Making Beer*, revised edition. New York, NY: Alfred A. Knopf, Inc. & Toronto, Canada: Random House of Canada, Ltd, 1994.

Miller, Dave. *Dave Miller's Homebrewing Guide*. Pownal, VT: Story Publishing, 1995.

Mosher, Randy. *The Brewer's Companion*. Seattle, WA: Alephenalia Publications, 1995.

Owens, Bill. *How to Build a Small Brewery: Draft Beer in Ten Days*, third edition. Ann Arbor, MI: G. W. Kent, Inc., 1992.

Papazian, Charlie. *The Home Brewer's Companion*. New York, NY: Avon Books, 1994.

Papazian, Charlie. *The New Complete Joy of Homebrewing*. New York, NY: Avon Books, 1984.

Smith, Gregg. *The Beer Enthusiast's Guide*. Pownal, VT: Story Publishing, 1994.

Snyder, Stephen. *The Beer Companion*. New York, NY: Simon & Schuster, 1996.

Snyder, Stephen. *The Brewmaster's Bible*. New York, NY: HarperCollins Publishers, Inc., 1997.

Periodicals

Bach, Ron. "02 for your Brew." *Southern Draft Brew News* 4 no. 3 (February/March 1997).

Eames, Alan D. "Beer, Women, and History." *Yankee Brew News* (Summer 1993).

Eckhardt, Fred. "The Joy of Lupulin." *All About Beer* 17 no. 2 (May 1996).

Ensminger, Peter A. "The History and Brewing Methods of Pilsner Urquell." *Brewing Techniques* (May/August 1997).

Garetz, Mark. "Dry Hopping for Great Aroma." *Brew Your Own* 3 no. 8 (August 1997).

Jackson, Michael. "Bavarian Wheat Beers–an Accompaniment to Summer." *What's Brewing* 1 no. 1 (July 1996).

Jackson, Michael. "The True Meaning of Bock." *What's Brewing* 2 no. 1 (Winter 1997).

Jankowski, Ben. "The Making of Prohibition–Part I: The History of Political and Social Forces at Work for Prohibition in America." *Brewing Techniques* (November/December 1994).

Kavanagh, Thomas W. "Archaeological Parameters for the Beginnings of Beer." *Brewing Techniques* (September/October 1994).

Lees, Graham. "The History of CAMRA." *All About Beer* 18 no. 3 (July 1997).

Lodahl, Martin. "Malt Extracts: Cause for Caution." *Brewing Techniques* (September/October 1993).

Manning, Martin P. "Airing Things Out: Aeration vs. Oxygenation vs. Oxidation." *Zymurgy* 19 no. 5 (Winter 1996).

Manning, Martin P. "Recipe Formulation Calculations for Brewers." *Brewing Techniques* (January/February 1994).

Manning, Martin P. "Understanding Specific Gravity and Extract." *Brewing Techniques* (September/October 1993).

Mosher, Randy. "A Turn-of-the-Century British Account of Selected 19th Century Belgian Brewing Methods." *Brewing Techniques* (November/December 1994).

Rabin, Dan. "Secrets of Pitching." *Zymurgy* 21 no. 2 (Summer 1998).

Index

additives 56
adjuncts 20, 56, 87, 126, 134
aging 37-8
airlocks 26, 32, 38, 83
alcohol 51, 102
aldehydes 102
ale 14-17, 102, 126, 131
  fermentation 50
  recipes 118-22
  yeast 50, 51
alpha acids (AA) 21-2, 47, 96-7, 128, 137
alpha acid units (AAU) 47, 96
alpha amylase 45, 87
Alt 16, 131
American Amber 17
American Bock/Dark 18
American Brown 17
American Cream Ale 17
American Dry 18
American Ice 18
American IPA 17
American Light 18
American Pale Ale 17
American Premium/Standard 18
American Wheat 17
Apparent Attenuation Percentage (AAP) 99, 130
aromatic hops 46, 48-9, 96, 98, 128, 136
attenuation 51, 99, 130

barley 10, 11, 12, 40-1, 134
  two- and six-row 40, 45
  unmalted 56
Barley Wine 14-15, 131
Bavaria 11, 12, 46
beer stone 71
Belgian Pale 14, 131
Belgian Red 14
Belgian Strong Ale 14, 131
beta acid 47
beta amylase 45, 87
bicarbonate 105
Bière de Garde 16, 131
Bière de Mars 16
biscuit malt 133
Bitter 15, 131
bittering hops 46, 47-8, 96, 135-6
bitterness 97-8, 128, 130
black patent malt 43, 126, 133
blow-off tubing 63, 102
Bock 16, 102, 131
  American 18
  Traditional 17
body 40, 42, 43, 45, 56
boiling 21-2
boiling hops 46, 47-8, 135-6
boil-over 21
bottles and caps 26, 32- 4, 72
  cleaning and sanitizing 70-1, 83-4, 106-8
bottling and bottling equipment 72, 106-7
brewer's malt 45
brew kettle 21
brewpots 60-1, 80-1
Brown Ale 15, 43

calcium 104
calculated hop scheduling 61
California Common Beer 18, 124, 131
Carapils malt 43, 133
carbonate 105
carbon dioxide 20, 23, 25, 32, 35, 48, 105
carboys 37-8, 62-3, 70, 83
carrageenan 58
checklists 78, 79
chill haze 58, 69
chloride 104, 105
chocolate malt 43, 126, 133
clarification 38, 58, 69
color 40, 42, 43, 45, 56, 94, 95, 128, 130
conditioning 13, 23, 51, 75
cooling in 22

copper 104, 105
corn 56, 134
Cornelius keg 73-4
cracking grain 20, 42, 67-8, 88
crash-cooling 38
crystal malt 43, 126, 133

denatured grain 20, 41
dextrin malt 43, 133
dextrins 20, 87, 93
diacetyl 102
diastatic power 42, 45
died, grain which has 20, 41
Doppelbock 18, 123, 131
Dortmunder 18, 131
Dubbel 14, 131
Dunkelweizen 16, 131

Eisbock 18
El Niño Red 120
English Old Ale 16, 131
Entire 15
epsom salts 104
equipment 26, 60-76
  cleaning and sanitizing 26, 27, 70-1, 78, 80-4
esters 102
ethyl alcohol 102

Faro 14
fermentation 12, 20, 22, 50-1, 96
  aerobic 31
  ale 50
  anaerobic 32
  by-products 102
  dry hopping 48
  equipment 62-3
  lager 50, 62
  primary 30-4, 37, 38, 48, 50, 51, 62
  secondary 37-8, 48, 49, 50, 51, 57, 62-3
filtration 23, 96
  equipment 69
fining 38, 58, 96
finishing hops 46, 48-9, 128, 136
Flanders brown 14, 131
flocculation 50, 51
Framboise 14
fruit 14, 57-8, 124
fusel alcohol 102

gelatin 38, 58
germination 41
glass, cleaning and sanitizing 83-4
grant 21
gravity 96, 126-7, 130
  final 33, 99
  original 30, 31, 94, 99, 137
green malt 41
Gueuze 14
gypsum 25, 55, 104

head retention 43
heating equipment 66, 80-1
Hefe-weizen 16, 119, 131
Helles Bock 18, 131
history of beer-making 10-13, 46
homebrewing 24-38
honey 11, 134
Hoppy Gurkha's IPA 121
hops 11, 12, 20, 21-2, 29, 31, 46-9, 67, 96-8
  boiling/bittering 46, 47-8, 96-7, 135-6
  dry hopping 48
  finishing/aromatic 46, 48-9, 98, 136
  hop utilization table 137
  pellets 49, 98
  plugs 49, 98
  storage 48, 49, 96, 128
hot break 21
husks 20, 21, 41, 67, 87
hydrometers 26, 30, 31, 33, 64, 83

India Pale Ale (IPA) 15, 121, 131
  American 17, 131
International Bitterness Units (IBU) 48, 97-8, 128
Irish moss 58
iron 105
isinglass 38, 58
iso-alpha acids 47, 97, 128

keg conditioning 13, 75
kegs 73-5, 84, 108
kilning 41

lager 12, 17-18, 50, 54, 65, 102, 126, 131, 132
  fermentation 50, 51, 62
  recipes 123
  yeast 50, 51
lag period 50
Lambic 14, 131
lautering 21, 90-3
lees 12, 22
liquor 20

magnesium 104, 105
malt 10, 11, 20, 40-5, 54-5, 126, 130, 132-3
  dry extract 25, 42, 127, 133
  grain 45
  malting process 41
  specialty malts 41, 42, 43-5, 67, 87, 126, 133
  syrup 25, 28, 42, 127, 133
  wheat 45
Malt Liquor 18
Marzen 51, 126, 132
mashing 20-1, 89-93
  decoction 87-8
  partial 61, 87-93, 126
  single-infusion 87-8
  step 87-8
mash/lauter tun (MLT) 20, 21
mead 11
metal, cleaning and sanitizing 84
mills, grain 20, 67-8, 88
molasses 134
monastic brewing 11, 14
Munich Dunkel 18, 131
Munich Helles 18, 131
Munich malt 132

oats 56, 134
Oktoberfest 51, 126, 132
organic acids 102
oxidation 31, 48, 49, 96
oxygen 31, 32, 50
oysters 15

Pale Ale 15, 40, 42, 54, 120, 126, 128, 131, 132
  American 17, 128, 131
pale malt 45
pasteurisation 10
Pasteur, Louis 10, 12, 50
Pilsner 12, 17, 48, 54, 123, 126, 128, 131, 132
  German 18, 131
plastics, cleaning and sanitizing 82-3
Plzen 12, 17
polyclar 58
Porter 15, 43, 122, 126, 131
preparation, importance 78-84
pressure regulators 74-5
professional brewing 20-3
pub, home 73-6

racking 38, 50
raffinose 17
Rauchbier 18, 131
records, keeping 27, 35-6, 37, 110-16
refrigerators 65, 76
rice 56, 134
roasted barley malt 126, 133
rye 56, 134

salts 20, 54, 55, 103-5
sanitizing 26, 27, 70-1, 78, 79, 80-4, 106-7
  water supply 55
Schwarzbier 18, 131
Scottish Ale 15, 121, 131
sediment 22, 33, 35, 38, 50, 63, 96
  on bottles and equipment 71, 82
six-row malt 45, 132
soda kegs 73-4
sodium 104, 105
sparge water 21
sparging 89-93
spices 11, 58
Steam Beer 18
steeping 41, 89-93
steeping bags 67, 81, 89
sterilization 80
Stout 15, 40, 126
  Dry 15-16, 122, 131
  Imperial 16, 131
  Sweet 16, 131
Strong Ale 16, 131
sugars 20, 51, 57, 87, 93, 134
  brown 16, 134
  corn (glucose) 25, 32, 33, 57, 134
  invert 16, 134
sulfate 105

tannins 23, 87
thermometers 26, 64, 81, 83
transfer tubing 63
Trappist Ale 14, 57, 131
treacle 134
Trippel 14, 131
trub 22
tubing 63
two-row malt 45, 126, 132

unmalted grains 20, 56

victory malt 43, 133
Vienna 17, 126, 131, 132
vorlauf 21

water 20, 54-5, 103-5
  dechlorination 27
  hardness 27, 96, 104
  mineral ions 54, 103, 104-5
  pH 103-4
  sanitation 27
Weizen 16, 40, 102, 126, 131
Weizenbock 16, 131
wheat 12, 14, 16, 40, 45, 56, 126, 132
  flaked 56, 134
  torrified 56
Wit 14, 119, 126, 131
work areas 79
worksheets and charts 35-6, 37, 110-16, 138-41
wort 3, 10, 11, 21-2, 30, 31, 54-5, 102
  aeration 50
  chillers 65, 82, 84
  gravity see gravity

yeast 12, 20, 22, 23, 27, 31, 50-3, 99-101
  ale 50, 51
  dry 52-3
  lager 50, 51
  liquid 27, 52, 53, 78, 100
  pitching rate 99, 102
  starters, preparation 100-1, 125
  storage 50

zinc 104, 105